D1568313

THE

WORK

OF AN

ACTOR

MICHAEL WOOLSON *On Technique*

Drama Publishers
an imprint of
Quite Specific Media Group Ltd.
Hollywood

Drama Publishers
an imprint of
Quite Specific Media Group Ltd.
7373 Pyramid Place
Hollywood, CA 90046
(323) 851-5797 v. (323) 851-5798 f.
Email: info@quitespecificmedia.com

ISBN 978-0-89676-264-0

Quite Specific Media Group Ltd. imprints:
Costume & Fashion Press
Drama Publishers
By Design Press
EntertainmentPro
Jade Rabbit

www.quitespecificmedia.com

Photos by Anne McElwain

TABLE OF CONTENTS

INTRO

Sharing your gift.

There is a lot of debate on what makes for a great acting career. Some think it's about a look or a magical *it* factor. Although that may be an element when it comes to getting a job, I don't believe it's the secret to a long-term career. Others say it's luck, or being at the right place at the right time. That can definitely play a part as well, but what happens if an actor isn't prepared when that amazing opportunity comes along? I can think of too many situations where people threw away their careers or disappeared after their "big break." Natural ability – which is often over-emphasized or used as a crutch – plays a small part in being a good actor. To be a great actor, however, takes tremendous effort.

When talking about a great acting career, I am talking about the people who stay on top, doing projects with integrity that inspire people; the ones who find deep connections to the characters they play, who make real contributions, and who seem to grow with every new endeavor. These people are truly rare.

You may or may not find this hard to believe, but most people who want to be actors don't really want to be actors, they want to be celebrities. They pose as actors because they dream of the attention it might give them. Most of these people don't stick around for very long and those that do are rarely happy. I learned early on that if I continued to feed my own narcissistic desires and need for approval instead of building a good relationship with myself, I would never find joy in my work.

Meryl Streep said, "So much of acting is vanity, but the real thing that makes me feel so good is when I know I've said something for a soul. I've presented a soul." When you are excited about great stories, creating characters and having an honest human experience outside of your own, you can genuinely call yourself an actor. To have a sense of value and a feeling of being in possession of a true gift though, you must have to have a good relationship with yourself and your work.

Although I strongly believe in the technique I teach, I don't believe there is only one way. I think most actors take from multiple sources and develop their own technique over time anyway. I myself was inspired by the work of Stella Adler, Larry Moss, Uta Hagen and many others. I encourage you to devour this book and take from it what works for you. It can also be a resource to go back to when you feel the need for ideas or information for a particular role. No matter what level you're at in your career, my biggest hope is that this book will inspire you to get excited about your potential as an artist and as a person.

I'm aware that there are some who are hesitant about using technique because they think it will make them mechanical or inauthentic. Don't think for a second, that I want you to act from a place of intellect. The tools in this book exist for one purpose only: to get you emotionally fired up so you can give dynamic, memorable, in-the-moment performances. It doesn't help to do this homework mentally if it doesn't bring you real emotions. You must never *act* a character but instead use these techniques as a means to deepen your work and eventually free yourself. Technique is a safety net when natural ability is just not enough or when the circumstances on the set are less than ideal. Shooting out of sequence is common for film and television, and the distractions are often enough to throw off even the most seasoned players.

There is also quite a lot of debate about whether real life experience or imagination is better when building background, inner imagery, and emotional work. There are coaches out there that are going to tell you to use only your real life and others that preach imagination. The truth is that every actor is different in what works best for him or her, so I use both methods in my coaching. There are fewer limitations that way. Your job is to delve into them both and find out what works best for you.

Above all, enjoy yourself. Find a platform to do what you love everyday and do it! Expanding your technique will often bring the passion back to your work and remind you why you became an actor in the first place. Great acting is about truth, connection and collaboration. It's about creating characters for the joy of the process. Take your work seriously but not yourself. People that happily give what they love are intoxicating to be around. So, get off your ass, embrace all you have yet to learn or master, face your limitations, find a coach who tells you the truth, and do what you came here to do. You have something unique to offer, so share it!

1

WORK ETHIC

The secret behind all great success.

If someone told you that the amount of time you spend working on your acting is directly proportional to the quality of your career, would you invest more time in it? Think about people in other professions who are at the top of their game and look at how much time they spend doing what they do. Compare that to the amount of effort most actors expend in order to be good enough to be at the top. Do they spend as much time on their acting as agents do at their desks? How about sales reps? Stockbrokers?

Michael Phelps won eight gold medals in the 2008 Olympics – the most ever won by an individual in single Olympic Games – largely because he has a relentless work ethic. When training, he swims for hours a day, every day of the year, including Christmas. Tiger Woods played fifteen years of golf before he became the youngest winner of the Amateur Championship. It's widely known that even after winning several world championships, he redeveloped his swing twice because that's what it took for him to keep improving. The very same principal applies to actors. Too many think they can avoid hard work and still have a chance to play great roles with the best. It just doesn't happen. People at the top of their game don't want to work with people who don't put in the effort; they want to work with people on their level. I'm not much of a sports guy, but I know enough to realize that Serena Williams probably wouldn't want to play tennis with me. Well, maybe a pity round.

There's a lot of talk about self-confidence in show business but I don't think people fully understand what it is. Confidence is merely the feeling that you can rely on something or someone which, in the case of self-confidence, is yourself. Where does true self-confidence come from? From doing the things you say you're going to do, finishing things you start, and having real skills. Don't just talk about projects; dive in. Even when you don't have auditions or acting work, spend time on great material in a class or on your own. Doing so will reaffirm that you are a creative person first and foremost.

The problem is that most actors are in fantasy. They think they can rely on their looks, charm, or natural talent. No matter how many of these traits you have, you will inevitably come across a character that will be out of your reach and the role will go to someone whose ability has surpassed yours. Despite the smoke that's blown in this business, the artists who are dedicated to working on themselves and their craft and who make real contributions are the ones who often have long, successful careers. So let's get out of fantasyland.

If any of the following sentences describe you, you may be in fantasy:

- You're not working daily on your personal and professional weaknesses. For instance, some actors may be able to express anger, but not vulnerability. Others are physically weak, have timid voices, or lack real technique.

- You don't have a platform to do the work – class, auditions, plays, a show, a film, etc.

- You spend less than two hours a day working on your craft.

- You don't finish the projects you start.

- You talk about your dreams of being an actor and don't back them up with actions.

So, how'd you do? Are you in a dream world? Maybe a little? Regardless, I think many actors are confused about what they can do each day to be productive and work on their potential as an artist. Reading this book is definitely a step in the right direction, but there are many other actions you can take to be proactive. Below is a list of ideas. Please understand that I'm not suggesting that you do all of these things now. It would be overwhelming and counter-productive to attempt them all at once. For the time being, just choose a couple that excite you and take simple actions to put them into motion.

- Work daily on your acting weaknesses. If you don't know what they are, find a class or professional situation that will expose them.

- Finish what you've started. Make a list and follow through.

- Make acting goals and be proactive about keeping them.

- Create situations that will challenge you and then show up for them prepared, on time, and passionate.

- Take a physical workshop like Alexander Technique. If you need to work on having physical strength, try kickboxing. If you're stiff or uptight, a hip-hop class might be the way to go.

- Write a script (short film, feature, or play).

- Produce or direct a play that you're passionate about.

- Get a camera and make a short with your friends.

- Read acting books that interest and inspire you.

- Block out a time each week to get together with fellow actors and read/present material that interests you.

- Sign up for an acting class and work on scenes as much as possible.

- Work on an accent that suits you and could be useful for future roles.
- If you're not going out on auditions enough, submit yourself for projects through *Back Stage*, *Actors Access*, and other reputable resources.
- Create a plan with a life coach or someone who will give you clear actions to take and hold you accountable to them.
- Take a voice class so you can vocally handle projecting, yelling, and highly emotional scenes.
- Raise your level of emotional intelligence by taking a psychology class or something similar.
- Improve your state of mind with self-help books, affirmations, meditation, yoga, etc.
- Improve your physical health and lower your stress level by working out and learning about holistic nutrition.
- Further reduce your stress by cultivating a spiritual practice that works for you.
- Learn a new skill that is challenging for you like singing, rock-climbing, a new language, painting, playing guitar, etc.
- Take an alternative type of acting class like improvisation, Shakespeare, or clown to gain a new perspective and challenge yourself in unexpected ways.

Do this exercise:

- Think of a career goal you really want.
    - What new skill could move you closer to it?
    - What class could you take?
    - What person could you model your actions after?

- What is one form of self-sabotage that interferes with your goal?

    - Make the decision to eliminate that sabotaging behavior and put a new thought process or action in its place. If your goal is to make a short film and you sabotage it by watching too much TV, make the decision to grab something to write with whenever you feel the need to grab the remote.

- Commit to an amount of time each day to focus on new strategies for reaching your goal.

- Hire a life coach or meet with a mentor to help you brainstorm new tasks that you must do each week. Make sure the person is supportive and holds you to your word.

Despite this list of suggestions, it's important to note that sometimes life shouldn't be entirely task-oriented. Occasionally, just being an engaged observer and watching people in a café, attending a concert or simply living your life can help make you a better actor. Just remember to breathe and enjoy your process, whatever that may be.

Resistance

Once you've committed to doing the work, you need to be prepared to battle the biggest villain of work ethic and passion: *Resistance*. It can come from many places and manifest itself in various forms. It has the ability to take you down and crush your dreams unless you expose and face it day in and day out. Steven Pressfield says in his book *The War Of Art*, "Most of us have two lives. The life we live, and the unlived life within us. Between the two stands *Resistance*." Without it, everyone would have everything they desire. It is a real force that keeps people from doing the things they know they need to do.

As a young actor, I struggled greatly with *Resistance*. Many of the friends I chose were often more competitive than supportive, they convinced me to do things I wouldn't normally do and involved me in situations I didn't care for. My *Resistance* picked those friends. I also made bad choices with food, exhausting myself with sugar binges and losing the focus I needed. My *Resistance* made those choices. It even lured me into romantic relationships that distracted me from discovering my blind spots as an actor. I went from one relationship to the next, addicted to that feeling of being loved or validated and, once again, avoiding the things I needed to be doing.

Resistance has even affected me while writing this book. It told me I shouldn't do it, whispering in my head, "You're a teacher, not a writer. Why not just take a vacation instead? How can you possibly say something that hasn't already been said about acting? Are you really old enough to be a purveyor of wisdom? Why not write a book later when you have more time?" In the end, the thing that finally made me begin this project was the realization that not writing it was making me unhappy. Now I feel joy and great satisfaction with the process, and that's reason enough to continue. We are so fortunate as artists. It's one of the few jobs that allows and prompts you to better yourself as you better your career.

Expose your own *Resistance*. It can take the following forms. Check any that apply to you:

- Drugs of any sort.

- Laziness or complacency – not working on your weaknesses everyday. I like to think of laziness as disguised fear.

- Mindless activities like bad TV shows, surfing the net, or anything else that zaps time.

- Unhealthy relationships. Some will cause you to lose yourself to the point of giving up your dreams. It becomes easy to avoid your own dreams when you're busy helping others with theirs. Other relationships may be destructive, unsupportive, or negative. Get away from these people. You may think you'll have fun or be able to save them, but it's far more likely that they will take you down with them.

- Over-working. Yes, it's possible to over-work. If you are someone who does, make sure to take breaks and cultivate other areas of your life.

- Staying in limbo on decisions that need to be made. Just pull the trigger and move forward.

- Going to bars, parties, or clubs too much.

- Speaking negatively about the industry. "I hate this business," "I was the best actor but they went with a name," "Casting people are all the same," etc.

- Disorganization – not having a space or desk for business. Your acting career is (Your Name), Inc. Would you hire a company that didn't have their shit together if there were millions of dollars on the line? Keep your environment in order – that means your work area as well as your living space. Staying organized sends a positive message to yourself and others.

- Avoidance. Face your fears and enjoy the rewards.

- Emotional problems you don't address. These spill into every area of your life whether you realize it or not.

- Spending time gossiping about or judging others.

- Being a victim. Remember that there are successful people who were older than you, less attractive than you, poorer than you, had fewer connections than you, or who had more hang-ups than you, and yet they still became successful. The only thing that is guaranteed to stop your success is victimhood. "Poor me" is deadly.

- Self-Abuse – hurting yourself physically. Thinking or telling others how you will never be good enough.

- Denial. If you're in denial, take off the blindfold today.

The bottom line is that the roles you're able to play are determined by your personal limitations and your willingness to work on the areas that are uncomfortable but necessary for taking the next step. So be honest with yourself about your limitations or find someone who will tell you the truth. That means admitting things that may be painful, but doing so will allow you to move forward. **Remember, life problems are acting problems.** I encounter people everyday who deny their weaknesses, and as a result, they stay in the same place. Then there are those who admit their weaknesses but make no effort to move forward. **Always remember that those who argue their limitations get to keep them**.

So, maybe you have too much fear, or passivity problems, or you're struggling with an addiction of some sort. Whatever your weaknesses may be, finding and facing them will bring you new freedom. This business can be extremely difficult and frustrating. As an actor, you'll be talked about both negatively and positively and you can't let either of those stop you from fulfilling your potential. If you overreact to criticism or let praise go to your head, you're putting your career in the hands of others.

So, what are you waiting for? Make your own success. Do what you can do to make personal and professional improvements so that when the opportunity presents itself, you'll be ready. **If you put in the time and find a platform to do what you love, the world will conspire to give you what you want.** *Resistance* is real. *Getting off your ass* is the answer to most peoples' problems. Just remember to reward yourself for a job well done.

Reward

None of the work in life is worth it without reward and celebration, which is why I tell my students, no matter how small the accomplishment, "Reward yourself." When someone has a breakthrough in class, I say, "Buy yourself a cookie." Why? Well, one of my favorite things in life is sitting down with my chocolate chip, chocolate-dipped, fruit juice-sweetened – because I'm hypoglycemic – cookie from the bakery around the corner. The truth is that any cookie will do, but those are heaven for me. They put me right back in my grandma's kitchen, when a cookie made me feel like the luckiest kid in the world.

So here's my question for you: what's your cookie? How do you reward yourself for a job well done in a way that isn't a form of sabotage? Going on a hike? Buying some new music? A movie date with a close friend? Whatever it is, it's your cookie and it will keep you going when times get tough or when you need to cope with the struggles that come with being an actor of any level. Treating yourself is a great way to avoid becoming bitter and angry. The last thing you want is to allow those kinds of emotions to spread into your relationships and career.

Casting – and anyone for that matter – can sense anger and desperation the minute it walks into a room. I define a desperate actor as the individual who walks in hoping the powers-that-be will give him a life by giving him the job. Instead, I encourage actors to come into castings with a full life and a passion to share their creativity – I'll talk about this more in the chapter HAVING A BALANCED LIFE.

Yes, auditions should be important, but when they become everything going on in your life, you're in trouble. Remember that even if you're rejected after putting yourself out there, your bravery deserves a reward. Take pride in your efforts and most importantly, have a sense of humor about it all. **Always remember that artists who happily express themselves and give what they love are intoxicating to be around.**

2

GIVEN CIRCUMSTANCES

The facts and clues used for building a character.

Consider the detective who tries to solve a mystery. He searches for every clue he can find. He looks at the relationships between them and draws conclusions. He's always open to finding something new. As an actor, you must be a master detective with your material. Comb the dialogue and the stage direction for the hints the writer has given you about your character and the world he or she lives in, look at the relationships between the facts and the characters, draw conclusions, and always be open to new ideas. This work is known as finding the **given circumstances**, and it's the first and most significant step of **script analysis**. Think of the **given circumstances** as the facts of a story the way a newscaster, journalist, or documentarian might present them. Research you do in this capacity will make up the groundwork from which you will build every character you play. It will also help you to deeply understand the motives of your character.

Doing this work may seem obvious to you, but I can't tell you how many people I coach – some amateur and some professional – who miss big facts in their material. I can often gauge the skill of an actor just by the condition of his or her script. Those whose scripts are clean and tidy are often slick and/or lazy actors who rely on their natural talent. Those with a lot of skill and technique typically have scripts that are written on and bent like they've done battle with them. These actors understand the clues I'm talking about and want to find as many as they can. In fact, I was once on the set of a movie starring Anthony Hopkins and discovered that his personal script was not only filled with meticulous notes, but also doodles and cartoon characters. It was as multi-layered as his performance and a perfect balance of work and play.

Let's look at the **given circumstances** of Lanford Wilson's play, *Burn This[1]*. Pale enters Anna's apartment from the streets of New York to pick up his recently dead brother's belongings. His hand is wrapped in bandages and he's in a rage. "Goddamn this fucking place, how can anybody live in this shit city? I'm not doin' it, I'm not driving my car this Goddamn sewer, every fuckin' time." His drunken, coked-out rant continues as he says, "What's that? ...Heat. The fucking room's an oven, bake pizza here, they turn on some heat." Anna says the heat comes on at 5am in the wintertime. She says she knows he's been drinking and asks if he's high, too. "Yeah, I did maybe a couple of lines with Ray, it don't affect me." "No, it doesn't affect you," she says with a dose of sarcasm. Later in the scene he breaks down crying several times about the recent death of his brother.

All of these clues help to determine Pale's **given circumstances**. His hand probably hurts, he's keyed up, he's feels like he's in an oven, he has been drinking and doing cocaine, and he's broken up about the death of his brother. These facts are not open for debate. When playing Pale, you can't walk into this scene casually without a bandage on your hand. Doing so would completely contradict the alcohol, the cocaine, and the events that took place before you walked

---

[1] Published by Hill & Wang, 1988. Published by Dramatists Play Service.

in the door. Nor can you act as if you don't care about your brother when there's clear evidence that you do. The fact that the dialogue is written with a clear New York dialect is also part of the **given circumstances**. These are the facts any actor must begin with when playing this role. Your interpretation, on the other hand, can influence his tempo, physicality, where to show lightness, when to reveal moments of vulnerability, and the different tactics he uses to get his needs met, etc.

When *Burn This* opened in 1987, the play received mixed reviews, but most agreed that John Malkovich's performance was riveting. He played the role of Pale like a non-stop hurricane. Frank Rich, a reviewer at the New York Times, described him as, "Combustible, threatening to incinerate everyone and anything in his path with his throbbing vocal riffs, bruising posture and savage, unfocused eyes." There was obviously a fire and rhythm to him that made him a sight to behold. Fifteen years later, Edward Norton took a shot at the role. All the **given circumstances** were the same, but his interpretation made the feel of the play entirely different. He turned the flame down a bit but didn't lose his drive. He found new rhythms and moments of tenderness that no one knew existed. In one particularly memorable moment, he smelled Anna's hair when her back was turned. Again, Malkovich and Norton had the same circumstances. Both were drunk, high, pissed about parking, and had New York dialects, and yet they gave entirely different performances. Both received rave reviews. Some people might argue that one performance was better than the other, but in the end, I believe that they both gave fully justified and creative interpretations of the same character. That's what it's all about: creating your own unique interpretation based on the facts given to you in the material.

That being the case, you must always do your best to get the full script for any audition you go on. Yes, I'm aware that sometimes it's difficult when you're busy with several auditions in a week, but do your best. Doing so will not only help you understand your character and their place in the story, but you'll also be able to speak intelligently when asked about it by a director or producer in a callback.

Ask yourself the following questions when searching for your **given circumstances**:

- Where does the scene take place?

- What time is it? What season? What year?

- Who is in the scene and what facts do I, as the character, know about them? What are my relationships to them emotionally?

- What do I, as the character, know about myself – my attitudes, my background – that is relevant to the scene?

- What do I say about myself as the character? What do the other characters say about me? Given what the script tells me, are those things true?

- How do the other characters treat my character?

- What literally happens during the scene?

- What events or conversations have taken place – or have not taken place – that are relevant to the scene?

Clarifying these details will help you build your character with specificity and originality, all while honoring the writers and their ideas. Going against the writer's intent is rarely a good idea and will often change the character or story in a way that dilutes or diminishes the impact you have on the audience.

Here's a critique pertaining to **given circumstances** that I once gave in class. The student and his scene partner were working on Neil LaBute's *The Shape of Things*.

MICHAEL: Okay, good, how'd you feel?

KYLE: I felt good. I felt like I was listening and being affected by her. I like LaBute's writing. It's how people really talk so it's easy to work on.

MICHAEL: Yeah. It was good work, very funny, but you missed something big. You know what it is?

KYLE: I have some guesses but I'd like to hear what you think.

MICHAEL: You look too much like *you* on any given day. You're too comfortable for this character. What's his journey in the play?

KYLE: She changes him into a cooler guy.

MICHAEL: Right, and the problem with how you're playing it right now is you have nowhere to go. You're too confident, your hair is kind of hip, your clothing is nice. You need to change your whole look so that it's a bit more ordinary. You need to come across as a guy that wouldn't get noticed much.

KYLE: Well, I didn't want to play him like a nerd.

MICHAEL: I don't mean wear a pocket protector and put tape on the brim of your glasses, but if you're hip at all, you're not honoring the **given circumstances**, which is an important part of the writer's intent. The end of the play doesn't work if you're too confident and good-looking in the beginning. There wouldn't be any build or arc. Right?

KYLE: Yeah, I just didn't want to be acty and fake.

MICHAEL: I get it, but you have to bring *something* to this guy. The play demands it. Your work was entertaining but there was nothing unique about it. Remember, you want to sign your work like a painter would. We need to see more of his character. He can't be comfortable. He's only had sex with two other girls, and that was in high school.

KYLE: Yeah.

MICHAEL: So get yourself some drab colors and change your hair a bit. Don't go over the top and create a caricature, but you need something. How about some dated glasses?

KYLE: I could get some old ones from my dad.

MICHAEL: Great. You also need to do some physical work for this. The way you carry yourself makes you look too strong and self-assured. Try rolling your shoulders forward a little and caving in your chest. Go ahead...... See, you already look better.

KYLE: This feels awkward.

MICHAEL: Perfect! Just standing that way makes you feel awkward. That's part of the magic of **physicality**. Play with that in rehearsal. Trust that you'll find a balance. Don't let your fear of going over the top keep you from trying things. If you play it safe, how's your acting?

KYLE: Not good.

MICHAEL: Right. Now, let's address how you might connect to the character's inner life. Do you have any secret insecurities that come up around women you're attracted to?

KYLE: Uh... yeah?

MICHAEL: Like what? (*laughter from the class*) Okay, we don't need to know, but it's an important question to ask yourself. Pay attention to how you are in real life when you're talking to women you find stunning. That's usually when those hidden insecurities come out. See how they manifest themselves, how the nerves affect your speech and vocal tempo, what sorts of behavior you go to or what you do to cover. Then, run the scene in rehearsal while thinking of your insecurity and see how your performance changes. You'll absolutely have new layers and new behavior. Right?

KYLE: Yeah.

MICHAEL: Okay. So find some more creative choices, play with your ideas, and go back and look at the hints in the play. I mean, listen: he gets a nose job for her, he loses twenty pounds, he says he's not good-looking or funny or clever, he admits that he was nothing until she started changing him. So let's see something she could change. Remember it's the first scene of the play. The way you are now you look like you should be modeling for a Gap ad.

KYLE: Cool, thanks. I'll do my best to be ugly.

MICHAEL: Yeah, sounds good. I want to see a different guy up there next week. A unique interpretation, but it has to be within the framework of the **given circumstances**. I don't want to see you playing a nerd or *acting*, but he's got to be average.

KYLE: I get it. Average guy is better than average acting.

MICHAEL: You got it.

This kind of exchange is more common than you might think. It is easy to miss, forget, or ignore very important information about your character and his or her journey in the story. As a result, I always recommend reading the script as many as three or more times. Doing so can yield new information and "Ah-ha" moments that make the process of creating even more fulfilling.

During my time as an actor, I sometimes struggled with finding the **given circumstances**. My own introductory lesson on this subject was with acting coach Larry Moss. One of my first scenes in his class was from Leonard Gershe's play *Butterflies are Free*. The character, Don Baker, is a very independent blind guy. The play takes place in his new apartment away from his overbearing, over-protective mother. Within a minute of the story's beginning, he meets Jill Tanner, a nineteen year-old, free-spirited actress who has already been married and divorced.

I really felt like Don wasn't too far away from who I was as a person, but the obvious challenge was to be believable as a blind person. I had never known a blind person and had no idea how they interacted with their surroundings, so I did all the research I knew how to do. Unfortunately, there was no internet at that time, so I had to go old-school: the library. I managed to find a book that laid out some behavior and I learned a few other tips by talking to a friend of mine who had worked at a school for the blind. After several rehearsals, my partner and I decided we had done all that we could. It was time to bring our scene to class and get some feedback.

Larry stopped us a page or two into the scene. To my surprise, his biggest note was that I was playing Don *too* blind. He told me to stop feeling around for things and just pick them up. He pointed out the pride that Don takes with being "normal," that Don actually says in the first act, "If you don't move anything, I'm as good as anyone else," and that Jill doesn't even know that he's blind until ten pages in when he tells her. Like so many who play this part, I thought the degree to which Don came off as blind was up for interpretation. However, the numerous hints in the play say otherwise. My homework was to go back and write down every bit of descriptive dialogue and stage direction about Don. This was a huge breakthrough for my work as an actor. It was so clear, how could I have missed it? The writer had given me all the hints I could ask for.

I brought it back with my newly discovered facts and the difference was night and day. That scene taught me something invaluable: writing down everything that is said about your character – whether by the character himself or by someone else, whether it seems important or trivial – is one of the most important steps in understanding the **given circumstances** and building character. To this day, it's something I require of all actors who put up material in my class.

3

SUPER-OBJECTIVE

The overall drive behind your character.

Extraordinary lives are filled with obstacles and heart. In 1991, at age twenty, Lance Armstrong won his first amateur cycling championship. A year later, he finished fourteenth at the Olympics. In 1993, he became one of the youngest riders to win the UCI Road World Championship. His success at cycling continued for a few years until, at age twenty-five, he was diagnosed with Stage Three testicular cancer. The cancer had spread to his lungs, abdomen, and brain. On his first visit to a doctor, he was already coughing up blood and had a very large tumor. His doctor gave him a forty percent chance of living and indicated that he would need chemotherapy to save his life. However, after two years of fighting the cancer, it went into complete remission and he got back into training. In 1999, he won his first Tour de France and continued to win for a record-breaking seven consecutive years; the previous record was five. Lance Armstrong is a great example of someone who fought and overcame every obstacle to achieve his life's dream: to be the best cyclist who ever lived. A great character always has strong desires, just as people with extraordinary lives do. Obliterating anything that stands in their way, they keep their eyes on their primary goal.

A **super-objective** – also known as the **overall objective** – is a character's want or dream from the beginning of a story to the very end and serves as the driving force behind that character. It brings consistency and purpose to a performance. The film *Milk* tells the story of Harvey Milk and his journey to change the ways of the world. His life is moving because of his drive to achieve his **super-objective**: *to win equal rights for gay people*. For him, it was even more important than his relationships; both of his lovers left him – one by way of suicide – because of his absolute determination to achieve his goal. Despite facing obstacles like lack of funds, fierce opposition, prejudice, and violence, he was eventually elected. Ultimately, he was murdered, but not before inspiring others and changing American history forever.

In the play/film *Doubt* by John Patrick Shanley, Sister Mary has a very specific **super-objective**: *to maintain the reputation and dignity of the school at all costs*. This becomes apparent in her first scene in the film where she walks past each pew, intimidating and shaming kids into silence. When she finds out that the man she already dislikes for his relatively liberal ways may be having an inappropriate relationship with a student, her **super-objective** bears its teeth. She uses the information to threaten him, turn everyone else against him, and eventually force his resignation.

Great performances have this kind of drive. Some even gain our admiration because they remind us that our dreams and goals are possible. Some actors want to take the easy way and not be clear about their character's **super-objective**. This is literally like going to the airport without a ticket or destination in mind. **A strong character has a strong drive and your job is to find it.** Sometimes your character won't be aware of his or her **super-objective**, but as the actor, you must be. Take the short amount of time required to make this choice, and your character will be clear to you and your audience. Even if you're only doing a couple scenes for an audition, I still say make a choice based on what little information you have. You'll often be given two or more scenes to prepare for an audition, and finding a through-line will add a cohesive element to your performance.

An effective **super-objective** is always derived from the **given circumstances** and is simple and selfish. Here are a few playable examples:

- To get married.
- To survive.
- To save my family.
- To be loved unconditionally.
- To create a safe place.
- To win the war.
- To beat cancer.
- To get revenge.
- To get him/her back.
- To find peace.

- To escape.
- To be validated.
- To be the best.
- To win my father's love.
- To be powerful.
- To have sex.
- To be rich or famous.
- To save the world.
- To find the cure.
- To have kids.

I am often asked if a character can have two **super-objectives**. Yes, but only if a major event takes place that changes that character's course. If your character focuses on business at the beginning of a story and then meets a girl somewhere along the line, his **super-objective** may change from *I'm going to be the most powerful man alive* to *I have to win her love*. In *Million-Dollar Baby*, Hillary Swank's character fights for the **super-objective** *to be the best boxer in the world*. Everything she does in the film stems from that desire until she sustains a debilitating neck injury that rips any hope of accomplishing her dream away from her. Her **super-objective** then becomes *to die*.

Personalizing the Super-Objective

It can be very effective to create an emotional link to your own life while doing homework on your character. If the **super-objective** you've chosen for your character isn't powerful enough for you, simply ask yourself what your **super-objective** is at this moment in your life and then link the two. It's unlikely that Hillary Swank felt a strong connection to being the best boxer in the world. It's far more likely that her personal **super-objective** had to do with her success as an actor. All she needed to do was to connect her life's goal of being the best with that of her character.

Let's say your character's **super-objective** is to get married. If you have no desire to get married, now or maybe ever, how do you connect to that? You ask yourself what you want in the same way the character wants to get married. Maybe it's to win your father's respect. Just tell yourself, "If, as the character, I can get a guy to ask me to marry him, my father will respect me in real life." You can have some fun with this method. Pick a personal, emotionally strong desire that will carbonate you and prepare you to fight, and then connect it to your character's goal. Don't play it safe; make it personal and the audience will believe it. If, on the other hand, you're already connected to the character's **super-objective** and understand it deeply, you don't need to personalize it. Do so only if you need to make it more powerful.

I once met the great running back Jim Brown. He had one of the best personalizations I had ever heard. Back when he played football, the sport was still dominated by white people. Since he was African-American, many players didn't even want him on the field. He said that when he went out to play, it wasn't about football; it was about bringing his race into equality. In his mind, the opposing linemen became the bigots who acted against his life's goal, and he literally mowed them over again and again to become one of the most respected running backs of all time. He has long since retired from football, but his **super-objective** is not far from what it was all those years ago. These days he works with gangs, trying to motivate them to put down their guns, make peace with their rivals, and become entrepreneurs who give back to society.

All great lives have tremendous drive and create change by obliterating any obstacles in their path. Find the deep human drive of your character's life and if necessary, connect it to your own. Don't fool yourself into thinking you can be general and make a weak choice or not make one at all. Your performance will suffer for it.

Note: When I say 'general,' I mean 'not specific' or 'lacking life.' When a performance is general, it often feels dead or flat because the actor has not made a clear choice. Good acting that moves audiences is always connected to specific choices that illuminate the text.

Do these exercises:

• Think of someone in real life who has an extraordinary life and determine his or her **super-objective.**

• Think of a memorable performance from a play or film and determine the character's **super-objective.**

• Determine your life's **super-objective.**

4

OBJECTIVE

*What your character wants from the
beginning of the scene to its end.*

In New Line Cinema's film *The Notebook*, written for the screen by Jeremy Leven, Ryan Gosling and Rachel McAdams play Noah and Allie, a couple in love in the 1940s. She comes from a wealthy family; his is poor. During one of his visits to Allie's home, Noah overhears an argument Allie has with her father, who loudly disapproves of Noah. Feeling that he's not enough for her, Noah walks out the front door, Allie following him soon after. She catches up, apologizes for her father, and tries to convince him to stay. Not only does he not want to stay, but he wants to back off from their committed relationship and just "see how it goes," causing her to fight for his love through the rest of the scene. Both characters try their hardest to get want they want. The result, in my opinion, is a powerful and riveting scene.

An **objective** is what one character wants from another character from the beginning of a scene to its end and is arguably the most important element of technique. Just as a **super-objective** gives a character purpose through the duration of a story, an **objective** gives a character purpose in a scene. It brings clarity to the character's actions and protects the actors from being self-indulgent by ensuring that they stay active. It's what keeps audiences in their seats. If characters don't fight for their needs, audiences get bored. Why should they care if the characters don't? There's nothing worse than watching a character be a victim or whine through a scene. "Poor me" is never interesting. You must always go for your **objective**.

Determining Your Objective

All **objectives** come directly from the **given circumstances** and are directly linked to the **super-objective**. If you think of your **super-objective** as a chain, the individual links are the **objectives**. **Objectives** help to answer the question of why any particular scene is in a script. Some are simple and apparent while others are more complex and require more detective work. You should be able to state them simply and actively. Avoid intellectual ideas that are harder to grasp emotionally as they will be harder to play and will get you into your head. Things like *to see that it's not right because your family hates me and you have money and I don't and I have to work and I can't go with you to New York anyway* just won't work.

Here is a list of some common, clear, playable **objectives:**

- Respect me
- Admit that you're worthless
- Go out with me
- Stop being a victim
- Have sex with me

- Admit you're wrong
- Tell me the truth
- Believe me
- Spare my life
- Beg me for forgiveness

- Apologize
- Validate me
- Admit that I'm better than you
- Leave and never come back
- Admit it's too late
- Go in there and give it your all
- Help me
- Look at me with love
- Say it's going to be alright
- Give me my power back
- Trust me
- Be my best friend
- Admit what you did was wrong
- Kiss me
- Love me like you did before
- Fall in love with me
- Be my biggest fan
- Give me my money
- Give me the answers
- Teach me to _____
- Punish me
- Give me a hug
- Hit me
- Do something naughty
- Dance with me

- Loosen up
- Be a rock star
- Be in your power
- Fear me
- Tell me what I want to know
- Fight to save this marriage
- Fight for me
- Make me feel safe
- Cheer me up
- Flirt with me
- Laugh
- Sit down and relax
- Save my family
- Give me peace
- Come over to my side
- Agree with me on this
- Admit I'm right
- Agree with my beliefs
- Worship me
- Treat me like a god(dess)
- Buy me a _____
- Make a fool of yourself
- Value your life
- Tell me I'm beautiful
- Ask me to be your wife

- Get me pregnant
- Tell me you're proud of me
- Say you love me
- Give me _____
- Make love to me
- Cut me a deal
- Treat me like an equal
- Do your job
- Convince me to not do this
- Buy this from me

- Take responsibility
- Set me free
- Fix me
- Tell me I'm beautiful
- Say yes to me
- Play with me
- Take this seriously
- Understand this
- See that I can't do that
- Stop loving me

Choosing Your Objective

People often ask me if there is always one right answer for what a scene's **objective** is, or if they have some choice in the matter. My belief is that while writers certainly have intentions for their scenes, you can make it your own. Once you've done all your detective work on the **given circumstances**, you can begin to phrase your **objective** in a way that triggers you emotionally. The **given circumstances** in *The Notebook* obviously would have prevented Gosling from going after *spare my life* or *admit that I'm better than you*, but he certainly could have chosen *forget about me* or *see that this will never work*. The idea is to find **objectives** that work within the **given circumstances** and to try a few of them before choosing the one that works best for you. Trying them all back-to-back in rehearsal with a scene partner will reveal the one that connects you to the piece and grounds you in the scene. When the cameras are rolling, feel free to try different **objectives**, but only after you've been assured that production has a good take with your favorite and most passionate one.

You may find that some full-scene **objectives** are difficult to figure out, but it's worth the effort to give a scene clarity and drive. In certain, rare cases, when doing this seems impossible, break the scene into two **objectives** that can either be stated together –*stay and love me* – or one after the other – *stay* for the first half, *love me* for the second. As long as what you find creates clarity and a strong impetus for the scene, you will be on your way to giving a dynamic performance. If, after mining a scene for clues, you're still having trouble determining your **objective**, a useful method is to determine what the other character wants. Your need will often be the direct opposite.

Phrasing Your Objective

Once you've determined what your character wants from the other person, it's important to find the phrasing that feels right when you say it, the one that makes you feel like playing the scene and changing the other person's point of view. The phrasing you choose should also be appropriate for the scene. Some may be a bit harsh; others may be too weak. Don't second-guess yourself. Follow your instincts.

I have found that there are a number of effective ways to phrase an **objective**. Let's use *Respect me* as an example:

- Please *respect me.*

- You have to *respect me.*

- I need you to *respect me.*

- I want you to *respect me.*

- I'm gonna make you *respect me.*

- I'm gonna get you to *respect me.*

- *Respect me.*

You can see how these seven options each have their own tone and size. Depending on the scene, a few of them will feel right, and a few might not. The same goes for *Forgive me*:

- Please *forgive me.*
- You have to *forgive me.*
- I need you to *forgive me.*
- I want you to *forgive me.*
- I'm gonna make you *forgive me.*
- I'm gonna get you to *forgive me.*
- *Forgive me.*

Some feel right; some are a little harsh, don't you think? So, the phrasings without **objectives** plugged in are:

- Please _____.
- You have to _____.
- I need you to_____.
- I want you to _____.
- I'm gonna make you_____.
- I'm gonna get you to _____.
- _____. (Simply state the **objective** by itself.)

Again, find an appropriate **objective** for your scene and plug it into the phrasing that triggers an emotional reaction in you when you say it.

Testing Your Objective

Once you've come up with some ideas for a scene's **objective**, there are a few questions you should always ask yourself. The first is if it has to do with getting something *from* the other person. **Objectives** like *I want to tell him what happened to me* don't work because you won't have to fight for it. Just tell him and you're done. You have to want validation from him, or for him to help you, or *something* that requires him to *do* or *say* something. Your **objective** should always demand a response from the other person.

The second question to ask yourself is, "If I get what I need, will it be enough?" If the love of your life is about to marry someone else, *Don't marry him* is certainly something you want, but if the person just says, "Fine. I won't marry him," is that enough? Probably not. It's more likely that the **objective** *tell me you want me instead* is closer to what you really want.

"There Is No Objective"

Never believe this, whether it comes from a teacher, director, or your own head. If it's a good script, all scenes have **objectives** or else the writer wouldn't have written them. Once again, **objectives** exist to give you purpose and clarity in a scene. Yes, there are simple scenes that you can overcomplicate by thinking *too much* about the **objective**, but don't buy into generality. Let me first address those moments when "There is no **objective**" comes from your own head. Sometimes students of mine will tell me they don't have an **objective** because their character doesn't want to be there, to which I say, "Then leave." Saying that you don't want to be there doesn't work unless you're being held captive against your will. Otherwise, it's a weak choice because it doesn't give the scene a reason for existing. When people just want to leave, they leave. They don't stand around and talk.

Characters don't want to leave until they get their needs met. Even in cases where characters run out and slam the door, there's typically a need to have the person run after them or feel guilty. Isn't it true that the drama of your exit is typically for the other person? Slamming doors, screaming something as you leave, or getting into your car and speeding off are all examples of that. Again, there is a reason the writer wrote your character into the scene. That reason is the **objective** and it is yours to find.

If a director or teacher tells you there is no **objective**, they may be trying to say, "You're pushing it, so back off a bit." If this is the case, or if they actually do say, "You're pushing," it's likely because you are driving the **objective** too hard. You must always be aware that over-playing an **objective** will look like *acting* rather than *living*, which is never good. Most people aren't aware that they push their needs until someone tells them, and then it usually takes some time for them to develop a gauge that will allow them to find the balance between under-playing and over-playing. I often tell clients, "I can see that you have an **objective**. Now stop trying to show it to me."

Always find an objective; just don't push or force it.

Personalizing the Objective

A good tool for rehearsal – along with exploring **objectives** – is to personalize your need just like you would with the **super-objective** by linking something you want in your **real life** to the scene. **Objectives** from your life that you failed to achieve often make for the most effective choices. Using an unresolved issue like this can serve to make an **objective** more emotionally intense for you.

Let's take another look at Hillary Swank's role of Maggie in *Million-Dollar Baby*. Early on in the film, she comes to Clint Eastwood's character, Frankie, with the **objective** *I'm gonna get you to train me*. She is met with his opposing **objective**, which could be something like, *I can't train you* or *I won't train you* or *I'm gonna get you to see I don't train girls*. If you were playing Maggie, you could ask yourself what you want in the same way that she wants his training. Maybe the answer is, *for that agent to sign me.* In rehearsal, try telling yourself, "If I can get the person I'm reading with to train me, the agent will sign me." Or maybe you have a pet with a life-threatening illness, so you tell yourself, "If I can get him to train me, my dog will be healed." Simply look at the character's **objective,** make a choice on how to relate it to your own life, and try it out. It may be just the trick to finding new behavior and opening up a scene for yourself.

Ideally, you'll use this tool for getting connected in rehearsal only. Once you're on set, it's best to focus on and be present with your partner, trusting that you have it. Only go back to this work during performance if you don't feel connected or if you need a little boost during your prep for the scene.

Driving the Objective

For that scene in *The Notebook,* Gosling and McAdams must have come up with something like *see that you're better off without me* and *stay and love me.* If McAdams had just *kind of* wanted what she wanted, it would have been boring. If Gosling simply would have *preferred* her to agree with him, the audience wouldn't have cared too much. As it happened, however, they both wanted *desperately* to have it their way. He fights her on the issue with all his might and she abolishes every argument. The **objectives** here propel the scene so powerfully that a place to breathe is difficult to find.

Allie wants what she wants so badly, in fact, that she eventually demands that Noah be a man and just break up with her, saying, "Do it! Do it! Do it right now!" She even goes so far as to slap him and end the relationship herself, saying, "It's over. No, don't touch me. I hate you. I hate you." This brings me to another important point: people don't always say what they mean. She behaves so harshly toward him in an attempt to provoke him into staying. If she really wanted him to leave, she would have just said goodbye and walked back into the house. But even when he drives away, she still yells after him, trying to get him to stay: "No, no, just wait a minute. We're not really breaking up, are we? Come on. This is just a fight we're having and tomorrow it will be like it never happened, right?" So powerful is her need that she tries everything she can think of, never stopping, even as he drives away.

Multi-Person Scenes

When working on a scene where your character interacts with more than one person, you have a couple of different options for **objective**.

The simplest way is to choose a **focus objective.** You must first figure out who your character is focused on most in the scene, then figure out what you want from that person. Everyone else will either be for or against you. If there are only two or three other people in the scene, you can consider giving yourself an **objective** for each person.

Another option is to choose a single **objective** for everyone, which is particularly useful when presented with a scene where you speak to a crowd of people. What do you want from them? To get out there and vote for you? Know that you're innocent of the charges? Rally behind you? When you know what that is, go after it, paying particular attention to those who offer you the most resistance and those who are most supportive. Regardless of the number of people you're addressing in a scene, **objectives** are a necessary tool for powerful performances.

5

STAKES

How far will you go to get what you want?

It's difficult to capture and hold the attention of busy New Yorkers walking down the street, but a man named Phillipe Petit managed to. In his documentary, *Man on Wire*, he snuck into the World Trade Center and walked across a high wire from the rooftop of one Twin Tower to the next. This was a life and death event, and it stopped people in their tracks. Why? Because we love to watch high **stakes**, and these were some of the highest New Yorkers had ever seen at that time. Imagine seeing this guy balancing on a wire over a hundred stories off the ground. Would you take your eyes off him for even a second? His success would mean accomplishing a near-impossible feat that no one in the world had ever managed. Failure surely would have meant death. This is a fantastic example of **stakes**. When working on a role, you must ask yourself what will happen if your character doesn't get what he or she wants. The **stakes** in a film won't always stay as high as Petit's throughout, but underneath the actions of each great character are **objectives** and high **stakes**.

A young kid is tormented by his peer group, so he grabs his dad's shotgun, walks into his school, and kills twelve people before killing himself.

A father wants fame so badly that he stages a publicity stunt where he sends a huge balloon into the air and calls 911, freaking out about how his son is inside, when actually the little boy is in on the hoax and hiding in the attic.

After a horrible accident, a mother lifts the 4000-pound car that's pinning her son to the pavement.

We all know these stories. People go to incredible lengths to get what they want, whether heroic, tragic, or somewhere in between, but why? What's at stake for them?

As an actor, you must always choose that your character cares about the **objective**. Otherwise, it's just not interesting. Usually, even if it seems like characters don't care, they're just pretending not to. I repeat: it's not interesting to watch someone who just *kind of* wants something or would *sort of prefer* to get it. It has to mean something. The more it means, the higher the **stakes** will be, and the more your audience will want to watch it.

Don't Be Casual

One of the talents required of being a great actor is knowing when the stakes are high and when they're not. If you're dealing with a simple, flirty, walk-and-talk scene between two people, it wouldn't be in your best interest to over-think the conversation and make it life-and-death. However, if you're in a high-stakes scene, don't make the mistake of playing it safe or being casual.

Two students in my class were working on the play *Middle of the Night* by Paddy Chayefsky. The guy was fairly new to class and was dealing with some resistance to technique and its importance. His portion of the critique ended up being about **objectives**, **stakes**, and choosing to care.

MICHAEL: Okay, let's talk about this much of the scene. You're playing it cool, like you don't care about her.

SHAWN: I'm not sure he does anymore.

MICHAEL: But you have to.

SHAWN: He says he won't contest the divorce.

MICHAEL: You wouldn't be talking to her otherwise. Why are you here at all?

SHAWN: I'm just here to tell her she's making a huge mistake.

MICHAEL: Yeah, and that you're the one she should be with. You have to bring down her emotional brick wall and get her back. Your character is far from being okay with this divorce.

SHAWN: I just feel like, if this was me, I wouldn't care about a girl who cheated on me.

MICHAEL: That might be easy for you to do, but this is a different time and your character's life situation is drastically different from yours. If your wife cheated on you, you'd just get a divorce and find another girl, right?

SHAWN: Sure.

MICHAEL: See how casual that is? You can never be casual or you'll bore your audience to tears.

SHAWN: Michael, I'm just not into the whole fighting for an **objective** thing. It just feels fake to me.

MICHAEL: So you want to be cool and casual in your scenes? Because believe me, that is *really* not interesting. It may get you dates, but it doesn't work on the stage.

SHAWN: (annoyed but smiling) Alright fine, Michael. I'll try it your way.

MICHAEL: Okay, that's more like it. So this is your wife, right? You love her?

SHAWN: Yeah.

MICHAEL: You must. You've gotta find *some* reason to fight for her. What's your **objective**?

SHAWN: I want her back.

MICHAEL: Okay, and what will happen if you don't get her back?

SHAWN: I'll be hurt.

MICHAEL: It's not enough. Raise it.

SHAWN: I'll be ashamed.

MICHAEL: Raise it.

SHAWN: I'll be completely crushed, ashamed, and alone.

MICHAEL: Okay. Now, this takes place in the fifties, so getting a divorce is a much bigger deal than it is today. It's devastating and still taboo for most people. Not only that, but your wife is leaving you for a much older man, so what does that make you?

SHAWN: Weak.

MICHAEL: Worse. You're a joke. And for someone who's macho like this guy, that's a big deal. That would be a huge ego hit for him, a guy who spends most of his time on the road in nightclubs. And what will your buddies and family think about you?

SHAWN: That I can't handle my woman.

MICHAEL: Right, so I'll ask you again. What will happen if you don't get what you want?

SHAWN: I'll be laughed at.

MICHAEL: Can you raise it?

SHAWN: I'll be lonely.

MICHAEL: Ooo, that's good. Can you raise that? If you can't get her back...

SHAWN: I'll be a lonely failure of a man.

MICHAEL: *There* you go. That's more like it.

SHAWN: Yeah, that's big for me cuz I hate the word *failure*.

MICHAEL: See, I got you feeling something. That's how much you have to care. Watching a guy not care is like watching someone walk in the hundred-meter dash at the Olympics. Now, look down here at the floor in front of the stage. Here's your metaphor: you're a hundred feet up a cliff looking down at water and rocks and if you don't save your marriage, you're jumping. Get it?

SHAWN: Yeah.

MICHAEL: Good. Remember, if your character doesn't want to be here, the audience won't, either.

The scene started again and was immeasurably improved. **Stakes** can save performances; it definitely saved theirs. You just have to be a good judge of how high they are at any given moment.

A Final Note About Stakes

When I say you have to care, I don't just mean as the character. I mean as an actor, too. If you just *kind of* want to be a great actor, you'll probably never be one. If you think it would be *pretty cool* to make a living as an actor, go ahead and quit. The **stakes** have to be high for your life, too. You have to care enough to do the work and risk failure. You have to care enough to invest your heart and soul into a story. Something in you must have the attitude of, *It has to happen.* That's what it means to have **stakes** as an actor. Yes, occasionally people who are cool and moody get work, but it doesn't take long for us to get tired of them. So please, if you just *kind of* want to do this acting thing, save us all some time and quit now.

6

EMOTIONAL RELATIONSHIP

Defining and redefining your character's relationships.

The stepfather who raised you is an honest, sweet, supportive man who has always loved and respected your mother and treated you like you were his own. That is, until the marriage unraveled and you found out he's actually a backstabbing liar who sleeps with prostitutes and sent your mother to the hospital with clinical depression and an STD. Sounds awful, right? This happened to someone I know, and it's a perfect example of how specific relationships are and how they can become redefined in an instant.

In acting, your **emotional relationship** to other characters describes very specifically how you feel about them at any point in a story and colors your behavior toward them. All characters in great stories will have **emotional relationships**. These relationships often change and evolve over the course of the story. Defining the **emotional relationship** you have to another character forces you as the actor to be specific and emotional about the people who interact with you in the material. It's an extremely important tool in the technique that brings specificity and believability to a role and is often what separates a great performance from a good performance.

You don't have to know people for any time at all to establish an **emotional relationship** to them. Years ago, my father wanted me to meet a long-time friend of his named Steve. During a holiday visit home, my dad decided to surprise Steve and take me to meet him. His wife, Mary, answered the door and warmly invited us in. It turned out that Steve was at a movie with one of his daughters. I was immediately struck with how wonderfully kind and cheerful Mary was. She served us pie and welcomed us into their home. She shared a funny story about her son shooting a hole in the sliding glass window with a BB gun and told us about the gifts she had bought the kids for Christmas. I remember thinking, *What a great mom. What a great family these people have.* At some point, Dad looked at the clock and realized it was after midnight. Mary apologized for Steve's absence, and we decided I would meet him some other time.

When we got in the car to go home, I turned to my dad and said, "What a sweet, funny woman. She's one of the nicest, happiest people I've ever met." My father said, "Yeah, well things aren't always what they seem." When I asked him what he meant, he said, "That's not the only side of her is what I'm saying." I shrugged the comment off; my father was just being cynical. *After all*, I thought to myself, *I know what nice and open is when I see it.*

Two days passed and I flew home. The day after Christmas my dad called me and instantly changed my **emotional relationship** to Mary. "Steve's dead. Mary shot him." She was no longer a wonderfully kind and cheerful woman. She was now a psychotic, two-faced murderer who killed my dad's best friend.

Determining Your Emotional Relationship

When students ask me about building **emotional relationships** to a specific character, I tell them to brainstorm descriptive words from their guts. If they were to call the person names, what would they be? *Hilarious, beautiful, sexy, adorable, soul mate…* whatever the words are, they should be written down. If a character is in a wonderful relationship at the beginning of a story and later finds out that her boyfriend slept with someone else the night before, her **emotional relationship** to him changes, and words like *lying, cheating, betraying, two-faced,* and *heartless* may come up.

So, go through your material moment by moment and ask yourself, based on the events of the past and the hopes for the future, how your character feels about the person he or she is talking to. Start at the top of the scene and brainstorm descriptive words for the person from your gut. Let's say you come up with this:

- Self-centered

- Clueless

- Selfish

- Prick

- Poser

- Pretty boy

- Thinks he's amazing

Now that you have those, the idea is to pick the most powerful ones and use them to create a sentence that makes you feel something when you say it.

- *My ex-boyfriend, the self-centered, selfish prick who thinks he's God's gift.*

When you create a sentence like this, whatever it may be, just saying it should spawn a feeling in you. If it doesn't, create one that does. When you find the right one, it should act as a launching pad into the scene when you say it, making you want to jump in and get your character's **objective** met. Just as with every other part of the technique, building your **emotional relationship** should not be an intellectual exercise. It's meant to get you specific, creative, and emotionally charged enough to go after your character's needs.

Using Conflict

Be aware that the words you come up with don't have to be all positive or all negative. You can mix the two. After all, how many relationships do you have where you love certain things about a person while other things irritate you? Some examples:

- *The love of my life who crushed my heart and stole my money.*
- *A stuck-up, bitchy diva who I would love to sleep with.*
- *My super-cheap, airhead friend who has a heart of gold.*

I'll be discussing John Patrick Shanley's play *The Dreamer Examines His Pillow* more fully in the EMOTIONAL TRIGGERS chapter, but I find it to be a wonderful example for **emotional relationship** as well. In the first minute of the play, the character Donna enters in a rage. The **given circumstances** tell us that she and her ex-boyfriend Tommy have broken up, that he has been hitting on her sister, that he has lied to her before, and even stolen from his own mother. They also tell us that these two have an amazing sex life together. This piece of information is incredibly important for the actress playing the role of Donna. During a conversation with her father later in the play, she describes the experience of making love with Tommy, saying it's beyond pleasure and that it takes her over like a storm. She speaks of her own body like an ocean that can't hold all the pleasure and that when they finish, the sheets are torn and soaked. She's afraid to be without it, because everything else seems like nothing in comparison. She feels like she'll lose herself if she stays with him, but she'll lose the sex if she leaves him.

If, as Donna, you were to leave this information out when building your **emotional relationship** to Tommy, you would just play the fact that he's a loser who you hate for hitting on – and later sleeping with – your sister. You can't just say you hate him or don't want him back, even though she says that several times in the scene – people don't always say what they mean, right? You must incorporate all of her emotions about him. He is not only the biggest source of pain in her life, but he is also the only person that can make her forget the rest of her drama and feel alive. At the top of the scene, he's not *my ex-boyfriend Tommy, the loser who's been sleeping with my sister.* Instead, he's *my crazy, cheating, manipulative ex-boyfriend who takes me to heaven in the sack.* If you forget about the love, it won't work. We won't see the sex in the fight – sex she'll never experience again if she walks out. At the same time, if you're playing Donna, you can't forget about the fact that Tommy had sex with your sister. That provocative visual should be enough to drive you crazy.

So, you see how incorporating conflict into the **emotional relationship** can be extremely important. You must incorporate all the feelings of any given moment in order to convey the writer's intentions.

Substituting an Emotional Relationship

When you have someone in your life who closely resembles a character in your script in terms of the way you interact, it can be effective to make use of the **substitution** method. Before Donna's entrance at the top of *Dreamer*, the actress playing her may think about a boyfriend she once had who cheated on her and broke her heart but who she can't stop loving. This is sometimes just what an actor needs to get emotionally charged.

When looking for a **substitution** for an **emotional relationship**, ask yourself if the character concerned parallels anyone you've had a similar conflict or event with. Once you've found a person, it's as simple as taking a moment to see the face of that person before you begin. If you're supposed to be attracted to someone in a scene, you can carbonate yourself with that energy by envisioning a person you're actually attracted to before entering the scene.

It's important to note that once a scene starts, you must be present and work off the other actor. Going through the whole scene while thinking of your **substitution** will likely distract you from listening to and working off of your partner. Simply use it as a launching pad to get connected.

When reading a script for the first time, feel free to write any **substitutions** that come to you in the margins. Doing so can help you later on when deciding on your **emotional relationships**. It can also be effective to write down what relationships or personal memories you are reminded of while working.

First Impressions

The minute you meet someone in life, you establish an **emotional relationship**. Think about being set up on a blind date. The moment you meet the person, you create your opinions. *He's cute, but not really my type. I'm in trouble, he's my girlfriend's type, not mine. Too fat. Too skinny. Too tough. Not tough enough. Too muscular. Seems funny. Sweet. Hot.* Life is never general. Only amateur actors are. So, even when you have a scene where you meet someone for the first time, you'll instantly create an **emotional relationship**. Even if it's simple, it will still be there. So, utilize this tool and build it. You'll be glad you did.

Do these exercises:

- Write out your **emotional relationship** to three family members or three close friends.

- Take a character you've worked on recently and write out descriptive emotional words and phrases that describe the way he or she feels about another character. Create your **emotional relationship** sentence and write it down.

Making Use of It

Most films are shot out of sequence and with lots of down time. An **emotional relationship** will give you a point of reference to start at any place in the script. It incorporates what just happened and all the history leading up to the scene you're working on. It can be all too easy with long shoot schedules – which sometimes become fourteen to eighteen hour days – and out-of-sequence filming to become discombobulated and forget that you had a pivotal moment with another character in a previous scene. Knowing your **emotional relationships** to the other characters will help you prevent this. Whether you're on stage, in a film, or on television, you can feed yourself an **emotional relationship** just before you begin. This will give your performance the necessary believability for illuminating the writer's story.

Instant Connection

Many actors find it challenging to connect to, and be open with, people they don't know, whether the person is a casting director or another actor. A very effective way of creating an instant bond or a feeling of intimacy is to endow the person with **shared events**, and there are two ways to do this.

The first is to choose difficult events from your **real life** and then to tell yourself that this person went through the same things. For instance, if in **real life** you lost your father at a very young age, you can imagine that this person also lost a parent at a very young age. Or perhaps you're someone who grew up with parents that were absent from your life and didn't love you. You may look into the eyes of your scene partner and imagine that they struggled with abandonment issues as well.

The second way is to take an event with heightened emotions from your past and include the other person in it. Perhaps you went through a difficult surgery in your **real life** and your mother was by your side throughout. You could simply **substitute** your mother with the person in front of you, remembering her as your support. Or, if you won a soccer state championship in your **real life**, you could tell yourself that this person was on your team.

I find it best to build two or three shared emotional events for each major character. It not only helps actors become connected to the people they're working with, but it also becomes powerful background for any role. Whatever **shared event** you use, real or imagined, be sure that it is appropriate to the **emotional relationship**. The examples I've given work best when your relationship is favorable. Obviously, if your relationship is unfavorable, you'll need to build accordingly.

Physical Interaction

Think about your current love, the last person you dated, a best friend or a family member. Those relationships prompt very specific **physical behavior**. That special handshake, a hug without touching torsos, a nose nibble, a slap on the rear, trading punches, a quick back scratch, grabbing your lover's bottom lip with your teeth, the 'kissing each cheek' greeting. All of these physical interactions say something about a relationship. Incorporating them into your acting brings credibility to your performance. In the film *Walk the Line*, Joaquin

Phoenix had very few scenes to help us believe his relationship with his daughters. In a dinner scene towards the end of the film, he takes a moment to tenderly kiss his daughter on the head. This simple moment solidifies their relationship in the minds of the audience, even though he does it to send a message to his own father that says, "You should love me like this." **The way you interact with a person physically conveys as much or more than the things you say.**

The bottom line is that you must always work to incorporate **behavior** that is truthful and idiosyncratic to the kind of character you're playing. **Physical behavior** with another person goes a long way in creating a believable relationship in film or on stage.

7

MOMENT BEFORE

Physical and emotional choices shaped by events that occur before each scene.

Consider this: your car broke down in the rain a mile from your house after your fiancé dumped you for someone more successful and better looking than you. Dragging yourself through your door, you notice that your roof is leaking again. This could quite possibly be the worst day of your life.

Now consider this: you dance through your front door after an amazing date and a great promotion at work that comes with full benefits and an amazing company car. You sing a little tune and dance over to the phone to share the news with a best friend. Life is pretty wonderful.

It's easy to see how different these two circumstances are. The point is that anyone who sees you walk through the front door after either of these events doesn't have to know anything about what just happened to you. They'll be able to tell how you're doing just by seeing you and watching your **behavior**.

The events that lead up to the beginning of a scene, along with the emotions and behavior caused by those events, comprise what is known as the **moment before**. The importance of this element of the technique lies in the fact that it creates the first moments of believability. It allows an actor to start a scene truthfully and it gives the performance credibility. Amateur actors start scenes from nowhere and come across like an actor entering a scene. Actors with strong technique bring specific **behavior** and emotions from the **moment before** and look like real people in real situations.

Every **moment before** should be supported by the **given circumstances**. When building your **moment before**, you must ask yourself these three questions:

1. What relevant events lead up to this moment?

2. How do they affect my character emotionally and physically?

3. How am I going to that place emotionally using my **real life** and/or **imagination**?

So let's go through them one at a time:

1. What are the events that lead up to this moment?

Sometimes the script will provide you with a specific **moment before**. Other times, you'll be required to create one. Did the character just get a speeding ticket? Walk in from a blizzard? Do drugs in the hallway outside? Get dumped? Run here after receiving a phone call that made her think her best friend was going to kill himself? All of these events would greatly affect a person's **behavior** and emotions.

2. How do they affect my character emotionally and physically?

Again, sometimes the material will tell you very plainly how the character is feeling, sometimes you'll have to figure it out, and sometimes your creativity will be required. If you just got a speeding ticket, you might be angry or sad. If there's a blizzard outside, you might brush the snow off your jacket as you enter or warm up your hands. If you ran here because you think your best friend might kill himself, you would probably be out of breath and panic-stricken. Every scene requires you to think about both your emotions and your physical state. Sometimes the answers are obvious and sometimes they require a good amount of homework. A client of mine worked on a horror film in which his character stayed awake for days because if he fell asleep, he would be killed. In one particular scene, he enters with the knowledge that a friend of his has been murdered, so his **moment before** involved heightened fear, sadness, and the exhaustion that accompanies sleep deprivation. Had this actor not incorporated those elements at the top of the scenes that required it, his performance would have suffered.

3. How am I going to get to that place emotionally?

This involves using your **real life** and/or **imagination** to get yourself to the emotional state that the script requires. See the EMOTIONAL TRIGGERS chapter for more details.

Hurly Burly

In the play *Hurly Burly,* by David Rabe, the character Bonnie returns to Eddie's house banged up and in a rage. She has been thrown out of her own car for smiling at her date and has had to walk to a friend's house. Her **objective** when she enters is to get Eddie to love her and tell her she has value, but as in all good dramas, she is met with resistance. Not only does he not give her what she wants, but he dismisses her pain and insults her, sending her into a diatribe. If you're playing Bonnie, you must solidly build the **moment before** in order to be believable. Your answers to the three questions might be something like this:

1. The facts: I was thrown out of my car; injured my elbow, rib, and knee; and had to walk to Eddie's house. Events I created for myself: I was solicited for sex and lost my wallet with my favorite picture of my son.

2. Emotionally, I'm angry, a bit embarrassed, and I'm trying to cover up the sadness caused by feeling worthless. Physically, my body aches, I'm limping, and I'm exhausted.

3. – again, reference the chapter on EMOTIONAL TRIGGERS –

It's easy to see how fully building the **moment before** will create an emotional charge with which to enter the scene. Without it, the energy falls flat and you can run the risk of losing your audience.

Auditions

Moment before is vital for strong auditions as well. I can't tell you how many times I've coached actors for auditions and they've missed the stage direction right above their first line that gives vital clues as to what they have to convey. As an example, an actor once brought me a scene that started with his character running into a warehouse with his girlfriend to hide from a murderer. When we began to read, it seemed like a normal day for him. I reminded him that his **moment before** was huge: he had been running from a killer and could be brutally murdered any second. In order to make the scene believable, he had to take that information and incorporate it, which meant launching into the scene out of breath, speaking softly so the killer wouldn't find them, and **triggering** himself into believable fear. All of these details needed to be incorporated before the first line had been said. Starting scenes from nowhere, like this actor did, almost guarantees no callback.

So what about **behavior** in auditions as a result of the **moment before**? My feeling on this is that you want to be subtle, yet specific. For instance, let's say your character is waiting for a lunch date. How might the **moment before** play a role in that? The first choice that comes to mind is to add some appropriate **behavior**. So maybe you check your phone to see if the person tried to get in touch with you or look in the direction of the front door to see if she's coming in. This choice is subtle, yet it brings us into the reality of what someone does while waiting for someone else, thus creating an interest for your audience even before the first line is spoken.

Playing the End

When talking about the **moment before**, I think it's important to mention that you must be careful not to play the end of the scene – or the middle –before you get there. I find that many actors will often indicate that something bad is going to happen before it does. This can be avoided by finding a lighter or more neutral **moment before**. When entering a scene where you're unknowingly about to get dumped, making the choice that you found a parking spot right in front of your New York apartment on your first try or that you just received a huge raise at work would give the scene somewhere to go. Just be sure your choice is supported by the **given circumstances**.

Incorporating Weather

Years ago, I was in a movie called *Alive* that was shot on a glacier for five months. The script required us to look cold in almost every scene since our characters had been in a plane crash in the snow. A fair amount of the time, it was as cold as you would expect, which freed us from having to remember to acknowledge it. When it's twenty below zero, it's not really that difficult to enter a scene and look like you're cold. Sometimes, however, when the sun came out and bounced off the snow, or when we were on the soundstage, it got hot enough for us to sweat profusely under all our layers of clothing.

At those times, it became really easy to forget about the cold and I often had to remind myself that I was freezing.

So, if you're coming in from the rain, you might brush the water off your coat or wipe your feet on the doormat so you don't mess up the floors. If you enter from a windstorm, you might need to fix your hair. If you walk into an air-conditioned house after gardening under the hot sun all day, you might wipe the sweat off the back of your neck and take in a refreshing breath of cool air. There's almost always room to play and the choices you make can create great **behavior** that will take your performance to the next level. Always look for clues in the script about weather conditions. Sometimes it'll be in the stage direction and sometimes you'll find it in the dialogue.

Props

For performances – not so much for auditions – it can be very effective to bring in a prop from the **moment before**. Walking in with a coffee from the shop around the corner, holding a parking ticket, reading mail, putting on clothing after sex, or multi-tasking with a phone and a snack are all great ways to help you feel natural at the top of a scene and to connect the current moment to the earlier one.

Time Jumps

It is imperative that you are clear about every **moment before** in the material whether you're working in TV, film, or theatre. In theatre, it tends to be easier to keep a grip on what's happening to your character from moment to moment, because every night you'll run from the beginning of the play to the end. You still have to keep an eye on what happens between scenes, however. Film and television can be far more difficult in this regard because scenes are often shot out of sequence. Sometimes you'll have to shoot the most climactic, emotional scene of the movie the first week of shooting and immediately follow it with a light-hearted one. The **moment before**, along with the **emotional relationship**, will safeguard you so that you can move into those scenes with believability.

8

EMOTIONAL TRIGGERS

How to deliver authentic emotions.

As an actor, consider how you feel when you read material with lines like this:

```
Chris slumps to the ground in desperation.

                    CHRIS
                  (sobbing)
        Please don't do this.
```

Scripts often demand that you reach a specific emotional place at a certain moment. What separates great actors from mediocre actors is that mediocre actors don't bring up real emotion, but instead fake it in their voices or try to indicate it with their faces. Other times, they simply push the perceived emotion in the hopes that the audience won't notice, or they'll just pass over the moment entirely. Great actors personalize and live fully in these moments. They make them specific with something real or imagined in order to deliver an authentic, moving piece of storytelling.

Trigger (trig'•r) n.
    an event or thing that causes something to happen.

                    The Oxford Dictionary of Current English

In the acting world, **triggers** are the mental movies, images, sounds, smells, tastes, physical sensations and any other elements that cause you to become filled with an emotion. At first, the words on the page may have little meaning for you, but as you do your homework and make choices, the words will begin to live, breathe and become illuminated.

Emotional Prep vs. Mid-Scene Triggers

Emotional Prep is the term given to a **trigger** that begins a scene. It is important to note that your **emotional prep** can be anything; it does not have to relate to the circumstances of the script as long as it produces the feeling. Mid-scene **triggers**, as the name suggests, happen during a scene and are most effective when they relate to the material. If you build a mid-scene **trigger** that has nothing to do with what's written, you run the risk of being distracted from the scene or becoming self-indulgent. A method that I call **overlaying**, which I'll discuss in more detail later in this chapter, can be a great tool for mid-scene **triggers**.

Oftentimes you'll find stage direction telling you to cry at a specific point. When that happens, you must work as deeply as you can on the moment in advance, and then trust that the homework will deliver the emotion needed. It may not come exactly where it's expected or with the intensity you had in mind, but who knows, maybe it'll turn out to be even more interesting. Do your best not to put pressure on yourself. What's important is to give yourself the most powerful choice, leave yourself alone, and let your **objective** lead the way.

Sometimes, however, you'll find one character addressing another character's tears in the dialogue. In such instances, the emotion does need to come up where it's specified, though not necessarily at the level specified. There's a scene from Patrick Marber's play *Closer* in which Dan fails to get the woman he loves back from Larry. Halfway through the scene, Larry says, "Don't cry on me." If you're playing Dan, you obviously need to be connected to something powerful for that moment, but you don't necessarily need to stand there with tears dropping onto the floor. The audience simply needs to see that Dan is becoming emotional.

Does All Material Need Triggering?

I often hear this question. I believe the answer is yes and no. Sometimes a scene is simple enough that a **trigger** isn't needed. Sometimes you'll connect to your material so strongly every time you read or perform it that **trigger-work** might accidentally put you in your head. The rest of the time, the answer is yes.

The next consideration is the amount of **triggering** needed, and the way to figure it out is to ask yourself, "Am I emotionally connected to this piece?" If the answer is "no," sit down, start building, and get connected. As I mentioned above, if the answer is "yes," you likely won't need to over-think your **trigger-work** (although it is beneficial to have strong choices in place so that if your natural reaction dries up, you'll have a safety net). Whatever your answer is, you must keep asking yourself the question over and over again as long as you're working on any particular piece. If the answer ever becomes "no," or "I don't know," sit down, build new **triggers**, and get reconnected.

Again, sometimes you'll be given material that seems very light and simple, and all you'll need is to know exactly how you feel about the person you're talking with. Make sure, however, that you apply the other aspects of the technique and explore your material as fully as you can. I can't tell you how many times clients have come in for a coaching and told me the material they're working on is simple, only to find they've missed something important and challenging.

Three Ways of Connecting

The following tools are ways to get specific about an emotional moment in your work. You might use only one while working on a particular character or you might use all three. Explore each of them in your work to discover which one works best for you.

Real Life

Real life triggers require the use of your own experience. This method is sometimes called **substitution**. The idea is to **substitute** a person, place, object, or event from the material with one from your own life. In a scene where your character weeps at her mother's funeral, you might visualize an equally painful moment of loss from your own life and then enter the scene.

This **substitution** method is particularly powerful for people with very rich life experiences. It also has the added advantage that it can be done quickly because there's less homework involving how you feel about the person, place, object or event. You already know how you feel, and you endow the moment with that feeling.

- Ask yourself, "How can I relate deeply to the given moment based on what I've experienced in my **real life**?"

Imagination

With this method, you throw yourself into the circumstances of a moment entirely, using your **imagination** to build **triggers** and background for all persons, places, objects and events. Taking this route requires time and research to fully develop mental movies that affect you emotionally. This means that if your character talks about a place in the script, you sit down and envision it, find photographs or paintings that resemble it, or even draw a picture yourself. Experience the sensory details: know what it smells like, what it sounds like, what pieces of it feel like, and what you may have experienced there. You put yourself fully into the character's shoes.

Daniel Day-Lewis is famous for doing this. People say that when he's on set, the story is his world and nothing from his **real life** exists. Clearly this technique works well for him. However, you must honor what works best for you. The principle behind strictly using **imagination** is that while experiences from your **real life** are limited, your **imagination** is boundless. In addition, some even believe this approach is healthier for the psyche.

• Ask yourself, "How can I build this moment and give it deep meaning by using my **imagination**?"

50/50

This method has also been called using an **as if**. It involves taking part of your real life and manipulating it with **imaginary** circumstances. For example, how you would feel if your real mother was diagnosed with cancer? What would it be like if you won the Super Lotto Jackpot? What if the most attractive person you know suddenly wanted to rip your clothes off and have sex with you? How devastated would you be if the most important person in the world to you were killed? These are all provocative questions that could bring up emotion when needed for a performance. Cherry Jones had this to say to interviewer Douglas Anderson about connecting to authentic emotions:

ANDERSON: How do you elicit emotions that you need in a scene when they just don't come?

JONES: As I've gotten older it's much easier. I found what worked with *The Heiress* – where I had several tearful moments – was the thought of the loss of (my lover at the time) Mary.

ANDERSON: That worked 371 times?

CHERRY: I could have used her every night. Some nights when I needed a break from killing her off, I'd use my family. I just need a springboard to get me to a heightened emotional state.

It's also very effective to use issues from your past, whether good or bad, and to manipulate them in order to make them more intense than they initially were. Let's say your character weeps over her dying sister in a scene. If, in your **real life**, one of your loved ones had a close call at a hospital and is now alive and well, you can simply tell yourself, "It's as if I'm back in the hospital, and this time they didn't make it." Again, you take a moment from your **real life** and apply **imaginary** circumstances to tap into the emotion.

- Ask yourself, "How can I manipulate my **real life** with **imaginary** circumstances in order to deeply connect myself to this moment?"

   OR

- "What could happen that would deeply connect me to this moment?"

Locating Moments

Now let's talk about locating the moments that require an emotional connection. If you're new to this process, this may be difficult at first. In time though, you will be locating them with no effort at all.

First, determine whether you need a **trigger** for the **moment before.** Then, go through the material and find any stage direction or specific notes where the writer has written a feeling – *angrily* – or an indication of a feeling – *she smashes a plate against a wall*. Third, look carefully for any other moments where there may be a transition of emotion. These most often occur when your character reveals information – *My father died last night* – or when information is revealed to your character – *Your mother has been in an accident.*

Determining the Cores

If you need to clarify or connect more deeply to a moment, seek to identify the **core emotion** and the **core event**. A **core emotion** is the emotion required in a specific moment. A **core event** is the event that occurs in a specific moment that **triggers** a **core emotion**. You'll find a list of examples on the next page.

Once you've found a moment that requires an emotion, you must ask yourself these three key questions, which are similar to those used for the **moment before**:

1. What is the **core event** by which I need to be **triggered**?

2. What **core emotion** might the character be feeling because of that **event**?

3. How am I going to get there using **real life**, **imagination**, or **50/50**?

*Note: Keep in mind that the **core emotion** you experience because of an event may differ from the one your character experiences. You must always pay attention to the clues in the text to find your character's reaction. If the character you're playing is in a small boat and sees a shark, your personal instinct may be to go to fear. If you character swam with sharks as a child, however, she might feel intense exhilaration.*

Lists and Examples

The following is a list of **core events** and **core emotions**. When you find a moment in the material you're working on that you want to connect to, this list will help you to determine the **event**(s) and **emotion**(s) that apply to the moment. Once you've done that, you can better look into your **real life** or **imagination** to find the **triggers** you need. The idea is to get the moment to emotionally take you over. For example, if your character's significant other has just had an affair, the **event**(s) might be abandonment and/or betrayal while the **emotion**(s) might be sadness and/or anger.

Keep in mind that there's no right way to do this and no right answer for a moment, but the braver and more specific a choice is, the more the audience will resonate with you and the more memorable your performance will be.

Core Emotions

- Joy or Happiness
- Sadness
- Peace
- Anger
- Embarrassment
- Insecurity
- Power
- Envy
- Excitement
- Awe
- Guilt
- Empathy/Sympathy
- Confidence
- Sexual Arousal
- Shame
- Disappointment
- Courage
- Humiliation
- Awkwardness
- Sweet Revenge
- Disgust
- Exhilaration
- Isolation or Loneliness
- Fear of Your Own Death

- Fear of Another's Death   • Anxiety

- Negative Shock (delayed sadness after an event like a car accident)

- Positive Shock (delayed happiness after an event like a surprise party)

*A warning: It is very important to understand that **core emotions** are results; results that cannot simply be played at, but will happen when using the proper **trigger** and a strong **objective**.*

Core Events

Dark Core Events:

- Failure– being fired, having a creative disappointment, failing a test, blowing an audition, a failed relationship, etc.

- Abandonment/Loss – death of someone close to you, loss of a precious item or keepsake, a loved one moving away, a break-up, etc.

- Physical Pain – being stabbed/shot/beaten, chronic muscle pain, a migraine headache, a deep cut or tear in your skin, extreme cold, being burned, etc.

- Betrayal – being cheated on or lied to, a friend sleeps with your boyfriend or girlfriend, someone you trust steals from you, etc.

- Violation/Abuse (sexual, physical, or emotional) – rape, a hate crime, verbal abuse, etc.

Light Core Events:

- Love/Loyalty– a special gift from a loved one, a romantic evening, a best friend comes through for you, a marriage proposal, etc.

- <u>Success/Gain</u> – getting a job you want, being promoted, winning an award, moving forward in life, a baby's first step, receiving amazing gifts or praise, winning a game, etc.

- <u>Pleasure/Beauty</u> – sex, a hot bath, seeing a beautiful sunrise, getting a massage, holding your baby for the first time, etc.

- <u>Humor</u> – a joke, a funny moment with a friend, being tickled, a funny gesture or physical behavior you witness, etc.

The Dreamer Examines His Pillow

Back to *Dreamer*. The play opens with Tommy sitting by himself in his apartment. His feelings of loneliness and being lost are so powerful that he's talking to his only friend, the refrigerator. Donna interrupts him, banging on the door in a jealous rage, ready to rip his head off. I've seen the play done many times, both on stage and in class, and it cannot be done well unless both actors are fully carbonated by real feelings.

There are numerous ways for the actor playing Tommy to approach the dialogue as he says, "Hail to you, Oh, my refrigerator. Is myself in you? Can this be real? I guess this is something I gotta exist through." However, it won't matter how the actor speaks if he isn't filled with authentic emotions. This challenge is further compounded by the fact that both actors must have mastered a lower-class Bronx accent.

Two actors new to my class attempted this scene. I stopped Brian, the actor playing Tommy, before the actress playing Donna had a chance to enter. The following conversation actually addresses the **moment before** for these two actors, but I'm placing it here due to the new terminology we've just gone over and the fact that every **moment before** is a **trigger**.

MICHAEL: Okay, let's take a look at this. How did you prepare for the **moment before**?

BRIAN: Um, I didn't really know what to do with it. I was just trying to be real and not push. I thought it was supposed to be kind of funny. I mean, he's talking to his refrigerator. And the scene hasn't really started yet, she's about to knock on the door.

MICHAEL: Well, it can be funny. This scene can be very funny. But it's not funny for the *characters*; it's funny for the *audience*. So let's talk about where he's at in his life right now, emotionally.

BRIAN: Well, he's been coop—

MICHAEL: Speak in terms of I.

BRIAN: I've been cooped up in my room for days, I've been sleeping with my ex's sister, who I don't even love, and I just feel totally lost.

MICHAEL: So that's a far cry from keeping it real and being funny, right?

BRIAN: Yeah, it is.

MICHAEL: So you miss your ex, right?

BRIAN: Yeah. I'm dying without her.

MICHAEL: Okay, so your core emotion here is loneliness because of your loss. So how are you going to get there? Have you ever experienced that kind of loneliness?

BRIAN: Yeah, totally. Not too long ago, this girl that I really loved broke up with me out of the blue and it really messed me up.

MICHAEL: So when you really miss her, when you're in the place of feeling that loss, what do you think about? What do you miss?

BRIAN: Oh, man, I miss her body, I miss being intimate with her....

MICHAEL: So how does it make you feel to know that you'll never be able to touch her again?

BRIAN: It makes me sick to my stomach.

MICHAEL: So think about a really beautiful, tender moment between the two of you right now, and know that that will never happen again… breathe… good, I can see the emotion coming up already. Now look at the fridge and know that it's the only friend you have left in the world. You've sunk so low that you've resorted to talking to a fridge. What do you want to do with it?

BRIAN: I feel like I want to hug it.

MICHAEL: So do it! And let the lines come from the feeling. That fridge is your only friend.

He began emotionally this time, pulling the mini-fridge close to him and wrapping his arms and legs around it, then laying back with it on top of him. It was worlds apart from the first attempt. Hayley, the actress playing Donna, knocked on the door, said her first couple of lines, and entered. Again, I could see that the **stakes** were not where they needed to be. I stopped the scene and addressed her.

MICHAEL: Okay, that was good, but the **stakes** need to be higher.

HAYLEY: I know, I *knew* you were going to stop me. After you talked to him I knew I hadn't been specific enough.

MICHAEL: That's fine. So let's get more specific. What's the core event?

HAYLEY: Betrayal. He betrayed me. He's sleeping with my sister.

MICHAEL: Exactly. So what's your core emotion?

HAYLEY: Pissed off and sad that he would do that.

MICHAEL: So, how are you going to get there? What experience do you have with anger and betrayal?

HAYLEY: Um… not a lot.

MICHAEL: Ever been in a jealous rage?

HAYLEY: No, I've always been a pretty calm person.

MICHAEL: Have you ever been competitive with another woman?

HAYLEY: Yeah, my sister.

MICHAEL: Have you ever had any blowouts with her?

HAYLEY: Yeah.

MICHAEL: What was the worst fight about?

HAYLEY: Oh, God, this one time when we were in college she lied to me and said some stuff behind my back to this guy I was dating.

MICHAEL: So do you have a boyfriend now?

HAYLEY: Yeah, we've been together for four years.

MICHAEL: Has he ever cheated on you or lied to you?

HAYLEY: No, not as far as I know.

MICHAEL: And, how's your relationship with your sister now?

HAYLEY: It's okay, not amazing. She's doing the whole corporate thing. Sometimes she judges me for how I choose to live my life.

MICHAEL: Okay, so let's do a **50/50**. Visualize what it would be like to see your boyfriend having sex with your sister.

HAYLEY: ...Oh my god, that's horrible.

MICHAEL: Yeah, it is horrible, how does it make you feel about him?

HAYLEY: Oh, I would kill him, are you kidding?

MICHAEL: Now visualize in your mind's eye a very intimate moment between the two of them, or see him doing something sexual with her that he's done with you... and know that they're keeping it a secret from you.

Her eyes began to well up with emotion.

MICHAEL: Now go backstage, visualize that picture, and when you can't stand it any longer, knock on the door with that feeling, and when he opens it, say your line and bust in like a Mack truck.

A few moments later, she pounded on the door in a way that told all of us in the audience that Tommy was in big trouble. She had embodied Donna even before she entered the room. That's a prep. Actors can try to get away with being general, but it just doesn't work.

Pitfalls

There are various ways that actors can sabotage their performances when it comes to this kind of emotional work. The following three traps are some of the most common.

Playing at the Mood

This occurs when actors play the attitude of an emotion – also known as *indicating* – with their voice, body or face. In other words, they *pretend* to have a feeling instead of actually having one. Examples of mood-acting include lowering the voice or using a whisper to indicate sadness, scrunching the forehead, frowning in a pronounced way, rolling the eyes, clenching the jaw, etc. These are all ways of showing the audience emotion, rather than actually feeling it. Some actors think that by mimicking a feeling, it will be perceived as genuine. What they're actually doing is displaying the *result* of an emotion, and audiences can often tell.

Some actors, even after becoming fully connected, still play at emotions. When the real thing is there, you never want to put anything inauthentic on top of it. If you're connected, we'll hear it and see it; you don't have to do more. Uta Hagen said it best: "Mood spelled backwards is doom."

Being Self-Indulgent

When actors get into their heads, trying to **trigger** themselves more than they focus on their scene partners and **objectives**, they often becomes self-indulgent. They can be completely emotional, crying profusely, but without clear needs, they come across like victims and the audience won't care.

Over-Preparing

While plenty of preparation needs to be done in advance, be careful not to over-prepare yourself on the day of the performance. The last thing you want to do is be emotionally wrought all day and have nothing left to give at the audition or on the set. The idea is to warm yourself up just as much as the material dictates. Before professional athletes begin a race, they warm themselves up and know when their bodies are ready. As an actor, you have to know yourself well enough to know when you're ready. If you're a beginner, be aware that it may take some time to develop that gauge.

Other Ways In

There are no shortcuts in this work. That being said, there are many ways in. Here are some alternate routes:

Overlaying

This tool can be very effective in boosting mid-scene **triggers**. The idea with overlays is to give yourself a powerful **trigger** of the same feeling as the emotional moment in the scene and then to tell yourself that the two are happening simultaneously. In doing so, you will create a kind of bridge that makes the moment in the script more intense for you. So, the moment you open the gift in the scene, you also win the lottery in **real life**. The moment your friend destroys your model airplane in the scene, he also destroys a cherished possession your grandfather gave you in **real life**.

To create an **overlay trigger**, first identify the **core event** and **emotion** of the moment you are working on. Then ask yourself, "What event has happened or could happen in my life that would give me the feeling required in the scene?" Let's say the moment in the film involves tears of joy after winning a gold medal in a race your character has worked towards for years. If you personally are having difficulty relating, or simply want to ensure the moment hits you as powerfully as the script requires, you have the option of using an **overlay**.

For most people, **triggering** into joy isn't that difficult. Experiencing joy to the point of tears is what makes this moment challenging. So once again, you would ask yourself, "What event has happened or could happen in my life that would give me the feeling required?"

Although the possibilities are endless, a powerful option for me would be to use a dog I had who was hit by a car in real life and died within a few hours of the accident. To this day, I wish that somehow I could reverse time and change the events of that day. So, a powerful choice for me could be to imagine her recovery instead of her death; to see her stand up on the vet's table healthy and strong again. I know this is an effective choice because the simple act of writing about it brings up the feeling I'm looking for.

The work required for an **overlay** is similar to regular **trigger-work**. I start by building the mental movie as fully, emotionally and deeply as possible on my own. Then, in rehearsal, I give myself the **as if** that the moment I cross the finish line is also the moment my dog stands up. So, I don't substitute or deny the fact that I am winning a race; I compound the joy with my dog's renewed life, effectively boosting the joy to a level that will bring the emotion I'm going for. I do that a few times in rehearsal by myself or with my scene partner so that when performance time comes, the **trigger** is in place and I no longer have to think about it.

You can use the **overlay trigger** with any moment you need help connecting to, whether it's a moment of rage, embarrassment, sadness, or anxiety. The steps are:

1. Identify the **core event** and emotion.
2. Find an event to use as an **overlay**.
3. Build the mental movie as fully, emotionally and deeply as possible.

4. Solidify it in rehearsal.
5. Trust that it will join you in performance.

Getting to Sadness from a Moment of Joy

Sometimes it can be difficult to go straight into sadness from a neutral emotional place. Perhaps you're working on the loss of a person. If the feeling doesn't come up when you focus on your **trigger**, try focusing on your favorite memory with them while telling yourself, "I'll never be able to do that with them again." Then, when the feeling comes up, engage your **objective** and move into the scene.

Using Loved Ones

When working on a scene involving the fear of one's own death, most peoples' instincts involve something happening to themselves without regard to others. I've found that including loved ones can amp up the power of a **trigger** significantly. Let's say a gun is being held to your character's head. Instead of thinking about your own mortality, picture your mother's grief when she finds out how you've been killed. See the tears that run down her face as she falls to her knees. Hear the sounds that come out of her. This type of **triggering** is particularly powerful for people who care more about their loved ones than they do about themselves.

Physical Triggers

While working on an emotional moment in rehearsal, be aware of what your body wants to do physically as a result of the emotion and your **objective**. That movement can be a good safety net for you on set or before an audition if you feel exhausted or if you've worn out your **trigger**. This phenomenon is known as *muscle memory*. If you have a scene where someone tells you that your father has been killed, your instinct might be to put your hands over your head and collapse onto the floor, or maybe to cover your mouth with your hands. That movement, in and of itself, can often bring about a deep feeling if you've connected it to the **trigger** during rehearsal.

Photographs & Films

Photographs and films, particularly from childhood and research, can help put you into a specific emotional place whether you're rehearsing, going into an audition, or on set. If you're playing someone who lived during a different time period than you, researching photos from that period may help you move further into the world of that character. If you're playing a victim of the Holocaust, watching a movie featuring real images of the depth of the victims' suffering might fill you with emotions and/or **behavior** you can use. You might even use a photograph along with a **50/50**. If you're doing a project where your character's mother is dying of cancer, you might look at a photo of your mother while thinking, "She'll never be here to see my first child."

A friend of mine owns a rare behind-the-scenes video for the movie *Dracula* featuring an emotional Gary Oldman going through his own family album before a pivotal scene. Only he knows what he was thinking about while flipping through his album, but those pictures clearly helped him connect to the emotional life required for the scene.

Unresolved Choices

Using an unresolved choice means choosing something from your **real life** that is still painful and not fully worked out yet. Examples include currently being in a fight with someone, a death that still causes you pain, or a recent public humiliation. As an actor, when an issue in your life resolves, it becomes more difficult to use. A good question to ask yourself is, "What are sensitive issues for me at this point in my life?" Those answers can be hot spots that you can use in your work when you need quick results. Be aware, however, that if you've been through real trauma and you feel you're not ready to use a choice like this, that you must follow your instincts and find something else. Be brave, but also be safe and honest with yourself.

Physical Pain

There are a few tricks that can help you exhibit physical pain. Perhaps your character has a headache in a scene. First ask yourself, "Have I felt this kind of pain or anything like it before?" If the answer is yes, go back to that feeling and get specific by remembering exactly where the pain was coming from – the temples, the forehead, behind the eyes, the back of the head, etc. Also consider how it hurt – sharp, dull, throbbing, constant – and what you did to ease it – rubbing it in a particular way, applying pressure, being very careful with the area, wearing sunglasses to shield your eyes from the light, taking a pain-reliever, etc. If the answer is no, however, you must build from your imagination by being specific in the same way and giving yourself an **as if**. You might say, "It's **as if** my head is in a vice," or "It's **as if** there are nails being pounded into my temples." Another way in is to transfer a pain that you have experienced from one part of your body to another. For example, if your character breaks his or her leg and you broke your nose in real life, you can move the memory of that pain to your leg.

Letting the Feeling Go

Some of the trepidation actors feel with this deeply emotional work is fear-based. They feel scared that they might have a hard time letting go of scary or dark emotions, which could then affect their personal lives. I believe that it's possible to do this work and walk away without any emotional residue. If you're having trouble letting a feeling go, try one of the following exercises:

1. Think of the emotion you would like to be feeling and **trigger** yourself in that direction. If you want to feel peace, think of a

time when you felt that all was well in your life. Breathe, relax, see the pictures and fill yourself with that feeling.

2. Take a walk or a jog, breathe deeply and with vitality, thinking of all the things that you're grateful for in your life. No matter what your circumstances are, there's always something to be grateful for, whether it be your health, your family, or even the fact that you're being proactive by working on your instrument as an actor.

3. You might find that you're physically behaving in a depressed way, saying "poor me" with your body. Putting yourself in the physical state of aliveness can rejuvenate you. If you want to feel joy, breathe the way you breathe when you're actually happy. Say the things you say or make the sounds you make when you're really celebrating. As cheesy as it may sound, open your arms wide, put a smile on your face, take a vibrant breath, and yell, "I'm alive and it feels good!!"

If you feel that you're still having trouble letting go of your emotions and memories even after doing these exercises a few times, seek a professional therapist to help you. Going to a therapist throughout my life has given me insight and inspiration to move forward through difficult times. I shudder to think where I would be today had I not had the courage to seek help when I needed it.

Lastly, know that feelings are just feelings. They do not make you who you are. Just because you feel crappy on any particular day does not mean you or your life is crap. Most people go from one feeling to the next, day in and day out. Be grateful that you can feel, because many people are shut off from their emotions. Remember that you've been through difficult times before and eventually felt happiness again. Treating yourself kindly, doing what you can to be healthy, and moving forward are key. Staying in life drama for the sake of your art is another form of sabotage.

9

INNER IMAGERY

*Endowing each person, place, object, and event
with a specific emotional background.*

It was a few days before Christmas at Franco Zeffirelli's villa in Rome. I was one of four young, American actors there for a screen test. Dinner began at eight. The table sat twenty and it was a full house. There were just as many staff members as there were guests and they were all moving around in a frenzy. Each time they came in, they'd bring a new dish and the guy in charge would announce it loudly and dramatically, "Pasta Carbonara!" There were meats, gourmet cheeses, breads, pasta with white sauce, pasta with red sauce, pasta with poultry and so many other foods I had never seen before. The aromas and the display were beyond belief.

Our host sat at the end of the table with a silver goblet in his hand like a king. His hair was gray with noticeable brown highlights. He was wearing a starched, bright white shirt with a crimson scarf draped around his neck and his teeth were stained with red wine. On and on we went; ten dishes turned into twenty. Was I the only one who cared that our call time for the screen test the next day was at eight in the morning? The large room seemed more like a theatre and I expected to see divas and tenors take the stage at any minute for a first-rate opera. The curtains hung rich and velvety with gold trim laced along the top. The dark, ornately carved wood paneling framed our dinner party and I felt like part of the set for whatever unfolded. Franco's voice rose and fell as he told his own stories and requested some from his guests. The gurgling sound of wine being poured was a constant backdrop to the mix of American and Italian accents that made up the conversations around me.

By midnight, Franco was beginning to look a bit disheveled. His starched collar stood straight up. He had taken his tie off earlier and had never bothered to put it back on. It remained crumpled on the table, half of it lying in a dish of lasagna. Everyone else was too drunk to notice and I gave up trying to point it out after two or three feeble attempts.

Dessert arrived. Franco surprised us, jumping onto his chair in a boisterous imitation of Pavarotti. He pulled two of the drapes toward his body, wrapping himself in the dark velvet as he belted out an aria from La Boheme, pausing for a swig of wine between phrases. He was very flamboyant and obviously felt free to do and say whatever he wanted. His audience clapped wildly as if this were the best performance they had seen in their lives. The other actors stood in awe like kids in a circus tent. I, on the other hand, clapped half-heartedly.

I was tired, distracted, and anxious, running the scenes for the screen test over and over in my head. It was now two o'clock in the morning and in my twenty-two years, I had never seen anyone as drunk as Franco and still able to stay on his feet. The marathon finally ended at 2:30 AM. As I hurried to the door for our ride home, he pulled me aside and said with his drunken, Italian slur, "Won't you stay for Christmas?"

As I write and think back on this story, I am filled with vivid inner images of that night, which is the focus of this chapter. **Inner imagery** is comprised of the pictures you see in your mind's eye when speaking or thinking about any person, place, object or event. For instance: the house you grew up in. When most people read or hear that, they see an image of the most significant house of their childhood. If you were to describe your room in that house, it would have very specific things in it. Maybe there's a favorite toy or a picture that hung on the wall. Perhaps there's a trophy, and when you think about the trophy, there's probably an image in your mind of the experience of winning it. The room itself has memories for you: some good, some not. Maybe you have a memory of your parents putting you to bed at night.

Movies like these are your personal mental images of a real childhood lived. You may laugh, cry, or become angry while talking about any number of these things. This is because they're real to you. Chris Cooper said, "You jot down ideas, memories, whatever, concerning your real life that somehow parallels the character you're playing, and you incorporate that in your scene work... The words, though they're important, are not the most important thing. And where I have so much fun creating a character is when I'm doing the homework – imagining, going on little head-trips. I love to fill my head with whatever I can concerning the scene and the character." [2]

When you read a script for the first time, you may experience **inner imagery** that moves you. If you have a script about a small town, you may think back and picture a small town you visited, or you may imagine what you think it looks like. If no images come up that connect you to the material in a powerful way, you've got work to do. You must make the writer's words come alive with your own personal experience or imagined movies. Why is this important? For many reasons, but the most important one is that **inner imagery** brings life to your eyes and connects you to the story, thus connecting the audience to you. When an audience watches you experience your **inner images**, it frees their imaginations to see their own images.

So what is your job? It is to build the images behind every person, place, object, and event you talk about. This will magnify the

---

[2] Jonze, Spike. "Chris Cooper." *Interview*, August 2003.

emotional meaning behind the dialogue and cause your performance
to have power and believability.

It doesn't help to do this work mundanely for the sake of being a
good student. Building stale images for the sake of fulfilling this part
of technique is a waste of time. Your images need to be vivid and
powerful enough to make you feel something. If your character raves
about a dog she played with on the street, you need to be specific
about the details of the dog. You can **substitute** a dog you loved from
your **real life** or build one from scratch, being clear about its size,
breed, temperament, fur, and everything else that applies, including
the memory of playing with the dog, seeing the way it runs, jumps,
etc. Without these **inner images**, your work runs the risk of being
general and uninspiring. **Your inner images must be emotionally
charged for you.**

In *Gladiator*, Russell Crowe gives history and imagery to two
small carvings, a process known as **endowing**. The carvings represent
the family that his character, Maximus, desperately wants to see
again, a family he has no real scenes with in the film. It isn't until he
finds their dead bodies that we see them on screen together, and in
that moment, it's clear how strongly Crowe built his relationship to
them. That relationship transfers into the carvings. When we first see
him handle the small figurines, he does so with tenderness and love,
kissing them with the sensitivity he would use if he were really
kissing his family. Not much time passes before the main conflict of
the story begins and he loses the carvings. When he gets them back
from Cicero later in the film, he opens the leather pouch they're in,
pulls them out, and his eyes fill with tears. It's as if he's finally
getting to see his family again, and all the joy of their lives and the
pain of their deaths flood his face. Djimon Hounsou's character sees
this moment, and after Maximus dies in the end, Hounsou buries the
carvings in the ground, placing his hand over the dirt as if blessing it.
"I will see you again, but not yet. Not yet." He looks up, his eyes
sparkling with the image of Maximus reunited with his wife and son
in the afterlife.

None of these moments would have been as alive as they were
without the work of **inner imagery**. The prop department gave Crowe

those carvings, and they had absolutely no meaning until he and Hounsou gave it to them. If Crowe had neglected to build his relationship to his family or left the carvings un-endowed, we would not have seen his love for them nor felt any compassion for his loss. Had Hounsou not done the same, the last line of the film would've been emotionally dead. Always remember that when dealing with a significant object on camera, you have a responsibility to build the imagery that makes the object important.

Just like with **trigger-work**, sometimes a script will move you enough to get you to the emotion required for dealing with a particular prop. If it doesn't, you must build your imagery. You must ask yourself what an object means to your character emotionally, and then find images from your **real life** or **imagination** to get yourself into that emotional place. Remember that it's not the object that has the power; it's the images and experiences associated with the object that give it meaning. If you've built the movies, they'll come up for you when you deal with the object in performance. Again, as with the rest of the technique, build it, trust it, and let it go.

In the play *Brilliant Traces*[3] by Cindy Lou Johnson, a distraught Rosannah DeLuce flees Arizona to escape her wedding, life and fiancé, Bronco Walpole and drives non-stop to Alaska. We find out later in the story that her father's Alzheimer's made him unable to recognize her at the wedding, which then woke her up to the fact that Bronco didn't really see her either. The emotional trauma of these moments motivated her to get in her car and drive to Alaska, eventually busting in on Henry Harry, a lonely, guilt-ridden man who blames himself for his daughter's death and has vowed to be alone and never hurt anyone again.

This play is extremely difficult for many reasons. This is one of those plays where not doing the work will result in absolute failure. The actress playing Rosannah must build powerful movies for a number of things, the most important being her father. She has several speeches where she goes on about how he upsets her. "I wanted to die..." "Someone can love you... can touch your soul – that's what

---

[3] Published by Dramatists Play Service, 1989

they can do – touch your soul, and then – bam – something happens and they can't remember you. After they've made in indentation on your soul. After they've dug into you so deep that they are a part of you, part of every cell, part of your skin, and under your skin, so that digging them out leaves you full of gorged places, routed out holes, disfigured, ruined, and alone." Those words are colored with deep mental images of watching her father suffer with his disease. These images must be built and felt deeply. Anyone who has ever watched someone they love suffer from this type of mental deterioration will tell you that the images run deep. "They've made an indentation on your soul," Rosannah says. Likewise, your images must do the same.

The actor playing Henry Harry needs images that are just as powerful. The memories of losing his baby girl must be horribly painful, especially because he assumes responsibility. At one point he goes into the details, talking about leaving her on the counter in the kitchen and then watching her fall to her death on the floor. This event, as you can imagine, would be absolutely devastating and needs to be built.

In *A Streetcar Named Desire*, Tennessee Williams' character Blanche Dubois speaks often about Belle Reve, her family's mansion back home that she lost due to funeral expenses. She also had to deal with the death of her husband, Allan. If you were to play this role, building the **inner images** of Bell Reve and your life with Allan are vital.

For me, the Hearst Castle comes to mind when I think about Belle Reve. It's a real mansion in California that still exists today, built by William Randolph Hearst, who inspired the main character in *Citizen Kane*. I had the opportunity to tour the castle several years ago and the images are still burned into my memory. The fireplaces are big enough to walk around in, the enormous indoor pool took several years to construct, and some of the materials for the ceilings were flown in from Italy. When I think of that place, I am in awe of the art of it, so using it as a **substitution** would be perfect for me. I could even combine it with a memory from my childhood when my dad rented a mansion. I remember running through the house with glee, counting the windows and doors and delivering the results to my father. If I had lived in a place like that my whole life – a place handed down through the family for years – and then lost it and moved into a shabby apartment, I would feel horrible loss and justification for staying in the elaborate fantasy world that exists in Blanche Dubois' head. Building those **inner images** of Belle Reve and Allan is not an option; it's a necessity.

In real life, there are images and mental movies behind everything significant we talk about. **As an actor, it's your job to make the writer's words your own by linking them with inner imagery.**

Building It

Just as the other parts of the technique, it's best to explore your options when building **inner imagery**, to pick the ones that move you most, and to leave the rest behind. Yes, sometimes you just need a simple image and it doesn't have to be deeply emotional, so use your best judgment based on the depth of the moment and the material. It's a good idea to circle all persons, places, objects, and events in your scripts to make them easier to find when the time comes to do the work.

*Note: As we move further into **inner imagery**, we'll run into some overlap with **triggers**. It's important to note that these overlaps happen in most aspects of the technique – just as **moment before** is a type of trigger – but it's still important to discuss the specifics of each element.*

Inner imagery can be built from your **imagination** or you can **substitute** a similar image from your **real life** for the person, place, object or event you're speaking or thinking about. It doesn't matter how you build the images, only that you do. Again, it doesn't help to just write some scribbles on a page. The images must bring up some feeling in you. If your character talks about a place that is special to her, you can either build it vividly from your **imagination** based on the **given circumstances**, or you can **substitute** a place from your

real life that you feel the same way about when working on the material. In performance, the images will meet you and you won't have to actively think of them. Once you've done the work, trust it and it will be there. If you find that your image loses its charge, go back and find something stronger from your **real life** or build something new from your **imagination**.

For example, if you're doing a scene where you're giving testimony in court about how you were raped and left for dead, you must personalize that event. If you have an event of that magnitude from your **real life**, it may be possible to use it. If you don't, you must imagine it in detail: where you were, what he did and said to you, the sensations, the sounds, the pain, what you did afterward, etc. If you build it fully, it will carry into your performance. **Persons, places, objects, and events become alive with importance when you link them to powerful images from your imagination or real life.**

Inner Imagery Building Blocks

The following are things to consider and questions to ask yourself that will help to make your **inner imagery** powerful.

Personalizing a person:

- Visualize three events that make your relationship to them what it is.

- How and where did you meet them?

- What personal songs do you relate to them?

- Did they ever give you anything, and if so, what? Do you still have it? Do you possibly carry it with you or wear it?

- What person do you have similar feelings about in **real life**?

Personalizing a place*:*

- See, hear, and smell the place in all its detail.

- How do you feel when you imagine yourself there?

- What significant events happened there?

- What real place do you have similar feelings about?

Personalizing an object:

- Where did you get it?

- Why is it significant?

- What does it represent?

- Do you still have it?

- How do you handle the object based on the feelings you have about it and the **inner imagery** in your head?

- If the object had a voice, what would it say?

- What object do you have similar feelings about in **real life**?

Personalizing an event:

- See and hear the event in all its detail so that it moves you.

- Notice who's there. See their reactions to the event.

- What event do you have similar feelings about in **real life**?

10

INTENTIONS

The methods your character uses to get what he or she wants.

"Bring more color to your performance." "It was all one note." "Can you make it a little more interesting?" "Boring." "I need more choices from you." "It was a little cliché."

These are all comments you don't want to hear, right? To ensure you never do, learn to use **intentions**. **Intentions**, which I will often call **verbs**, are the colors, the variations, the different ways characters go about getting their needs met.

When going into a job interview, you probably use a range of tactics to get the execs to hire you. When you enter, you might charm or sweet-talk the casting person. After sitting down, you might begin to befriend or humor them. Eventually you might try to impress them by saying something smart. You do all these things in order to get the job.

Consider teenagers and the many ways they go about trying to get that newest gadget. They might start by sweet-talking their parents even before bringing it up. When refused, they may move on to pleading, bluffing, and reasoning. When eventually they get pissed off at their parents, they may guilt, prosecute, reject, disown, and finally, they may make a last desperate attempt of threatening to run away. They keep changing tactics to get that gadget. It would be ridiculous to think that after being denied the first time, they would just keep requesting in the same way, "Can I have it? Can I have it? Can I have it?" The same is true for acting, but amateur actors don't make this connection. They often read all the lines with the same **intention** and hope to get a callback. It rarely happens.

Great actors, just like driven, demanding teenagers, try one tactic to get what they want, and if that doesn't work, they try something else. The same is true for great painters, who use a variety of colors to create a work of art. Finding great **intentions** brings color and personality to the work.

Intentions are also significant because they help to remove your focus from yourself and keep your performance active. They also force you to make choices instead of taking the easy way out and relying on your personality or natural ability. Choosing interesting **verbs** is one of the easiest ways to give powerful, dynamic performances. A list is provided for you later in this chapter.

To the Skeptics

There are some people that believe that using **intentions** is not a good way to work because they keep you stuck or closed off to the moment-to-moment work with another actor. Others say **intentions** get them in their heads and make them inauthentic. I say that if you can learn to use **intentions** as a rehearsal tool *only* and then find a way to let them go and be free to react in your performances, you will be a better actor.

Intentions are like the notes of a violinist songwriter. She chooses them carefully, tries different ideas and variations, and eventually chooses her favorite arrangement. She knows what the song means to her and when she begins to commit it to memory, she may go through it very technically in bits and pieces, but she keeps the overall meaning in mind. When performance time comes, all the notes are ingrained in her to such an extent that she no longer has to think about them. She can infuse the song with meaning in that moment, and if she's performing alongside other musicians, each of them will be influenced by the other's interpretation. The technicality will have melted away to be replaced by the expression of what the song means to all of them. **Intentions** work exactly the same way. They act as guidelines in rehearsal to build a framework for a scene and should be released in performance.

Intentions can save you from hack-acting. I've had countless skeptics eventually choose to use them religiously. Yes, you have to be open and not get stuck in the way you read a line. Yes, you want to really listen to your scene partner and react spontaneously. Yes, you want to be willing to let your choices go when a director asks for it a different way. However, when you have crappy co-stars that give you nothing, or directors who have no idea what they're doing, or when you read with that dead fish of a casting director, you will be glad you used **intentions**. They will be the safety net for your performance.

Shades vs. Colors

While some **verbs** can be thought of as completely different colors – *to attack* and *to befriend* – others simply represent different shades of the same color. Just as an artist picks out twenty different shades of blue, you can explore variations of the same type of **verb** – *to brush off, to dismiss, to reject, to deny*. This difference can be useful when assigning **verbs** to your lines – a process known as **verb-scoring**. Maybe one line is in the same color family as the one before but is a different shade. Then, when something big happens later in the scene, maybe you change colors entirely.

How to Pick a Good Intention

A good **intention** is active and specific while bad **intentions** are passive and general. Things like *explain, tell,* and *ask* are ineffective because they're generic and weak, as opposed to more solid choices like *excite, enlighten,* and *coax.* Most effective **verbs** can be plugged into this formula: *I _____ you.*

I tease you, I warn you, I interrogate you, I humor you, etc. Other **verbs** can be more creative, like *to brush the hair out of your face.* Brushing the hair isn't something that you have to physically do, but the energy that goes along with that is what's important.

Let's take the line, "Where are you going?" The obvious **intention** choice is *to investigate*, but what else is there? How about *to sweet-talk*? It gives some *hey, stick around and we could have some fun* subtext to the line. How about *to interrogate*? That's a little more like, *if you leave, I'll make life difficult for you.* Or *to scare*? This one might elicit a new, authentic reaction from the other actor. To reiterate, **intentions** are choices that an actor plays, similar to the way an artist mixes and chooses colors for a canvas. An actor without **intentions** is like an artist who only has white paint. Boring. Blank. Yes, natural ability can create some choices, but why limit yourself to those?

There are two particular types of scenes I want to bring special attention to. The first is the seduction scene. Most people I coach who bring in a scene with the **objective** *to get you to have sex with me* do it with the same **intention** all the way through. Even this type of scene can get boring if the actor is trying to play *to flirt with* on every line. The scene becomes much more provocative when they begin to explore other ways of getting sex. You can start with *to flirt*, then move into *to humor* when flirting doesn't work, then to *tantalize, arouse, tempt, tickle, sweet-talk, entice, caress, thrill, surprise, shock,* *dominate,* and so on, raising the bar as you go. Doing this makes a scene much more watchable because as you come up against resistance and up the ante, you will raise the **stakes** for the other actor as well.

Additionally, seduction scenes are often the most uncomfortable scenes to do. Women in particular tend to be shy about expressing themselves in this way in their acting. **Intentions** give them freedom. Regardless of your gender or comfort level, **intentions** move your focus from yourself to the other person in the scene. If you're committed to your choices, they'll even enliven your acting experiences by forcing you to be brave.

The second type of scene I'd like to discuss is the power scene. I think we can all agree that Heath Ledger's performance as the Joker in *The Dark Knight* was inventive and explosive. It has to be one of the greatest portrayals of a villain of all time. Yes, the character work was off the charts, but what can we learn from it in terms of **intention**. Most scenes where an actor is in power – interrogations, fights, etc. – are filled with **intentions** like *blame, attack, warn, threaten,* etc., different shades of the same color. Ledger certainly used those, but he went on to *flirt with, toy with, provoke, corner, mock, humor, hunt, annoy, dominate, coax, invigorate, tempt, beautify, surprise,* etc. The fact that his **verb** choices were so extensive is one of the biggest reasons why we couldn't take our eyes off him and why it's unlikely he'll be forgotten as an actor. He was a true artist; a guy who wasn't interested in celebrity status. He was more excited about how he could create and inhabit a character.

You get it, right? A great performance uses provocative colors/**intentions**. A mediocre actor uses boring **intentions**, generic **intentions** or just none at all. Don't be lazy; be inventive. It's much more fun that way.

The **verb** list starts on the next page. By all means, if you find a **verb** you like and want a variation that isn't listed, look it up in a thesaurus, which is a great resource for **intentions**. I've put the **verbs** into simple categories that make it easier to find the ones you're looking for. Remember to be open and try different choices to find the most effective ones for you and the material.

Dangerous Words

abolish	damage	incinerate	shove
anger	deflower	kill	skewer
annihilate	defy	knife	skin
assault	destroy	massacre	slaughter
attack	devastate	mutilate	slit
banish	devour	nail	smash
bash	dissect	obliterate	stab
brutalize	disturb	outrage	stalk
burn	dominate	penetrate	startle
bury	eliminate	poison	terminate
butcher	enrage	provoke	terrify
castrate	expose	pulverize	terrorize
command	exterminate	rape	threaten
conquer	finish	ruin	torture
crucify	horrify	sacrifice	vilify
crush	hunt	scalp	violate
cut	impale	scare	wreck

Encouraging Words

assemble	encourage	hook	propel
awaken	energize	ignite	push
boost	enflame	impassion	rally
champion	engage	impress	rejuvenate
clarify	enlighten	inflate	reward
coax	enlist	inspire	shake
congratulate	enliven	investigate	spur
dazzle	excite	invigorate	steer
drive	exhilarate	launch	stimulate
educate	fascinate	lead	stir
ego-pump	flatter	nudge	teach
electrify	free	press	unite
empower	fuel	prod	uplift

Discouraging Words

abandon	defend	humiliate	quiz
abuse	deflate	hurt	rattle
accuse	degrade	ignore	rebuke
aggravate	demean	impede	reject
agitate	demote	incriminate	repulse
alarm	denounce	insult	resist
alienate	deny	interrogate	revoke
annoy	deprecate	intimidate	ridicule
assault	derail	invalidate	sabotage
badger	detain	irritate	scold
battle	devalue	jolt	shake
beg	diminish	judge	shame
belittle	disable	mimic	shock
betray	disappoint	mock	silence
bite	disarm	muzzle	slap
blame	discard	needle	smack
block	discourage	neutralize	snub
bother	discredit	offend	stalk
bruise	disgrace	oppose	sting
brush off	dismiss	over-throw	stop
bug	disown	overwhelm	stun
bully	disturb	patronize	stupidify
cage	dominate	penetrate	suppress
censor	embarrass	persecute	taunt
challenge	expose	pester	tease
chastise	frustrate	plague	test
command	grill	plead	torment
condemn	guilt	poke	trash
confront	halt	police	trump
contest	harm	punch	undermine
corner	hinder	punish	use
criticize	hound	pursue	warn

Loving/Supporting Words

absolve	elevate	navigate	revitalize
accept	embrace	nourish	school
accommodate	enliven	nurture	secure
acknowledge	ensure	obey	serve
admire	entertain	pacify	shepherd
adore	envelop	pamper	shield
amuse	father	perfect	sober
apologize to	fix	please	soothe
applaud	flatter	praise	support
assist	forgive	promise	surprise
beautify	glorify	promote	tame
befriend	greet	protect	tease
bless	guide	purify	thank
bond with	heal	pursue	treasure
calm	help	queen	treat
clarify	hold	reason with	unburden
coddle	hug	redeem	unify
comfort	humor	refine	unite
compliment	idolize	reform	uplift
court	invite	rehabilitate	validate
cradle	king	relax	value
credit	liberate	release	vindicate
defrost	lighten	relinquish	welcome
delight	mend	rescue	worship
develop	mother	respect	

Misleading Words

avoid	deceive	dupe	misguide
bait	decoy	ensnare	mislead
bewitch	deflect	entrap	outwit
bluff	delude	evade	persuade
cheat	distract	fool	scam
coerce	divert	lead on	trap
confuse	dodge	lure	trick

Intimate Words

adore	entice	nibble	sweet-talk
arouse	excite	nuzzle	tantalize
beautify	flirt with	pleasure	tempt
caress	impassion	romance	thrill
coax	kiss	satisfy	tickle
cuddle	lick	stimulate	titillate
embrace	lure	stroke	toy with

Good **intentions** often engage the body. That doesn't mean you should be moving on every line, however. You can be completely still, but the instinct should be there. Sometimes a **verb** will make you want to physically go after someone; sometimes it will make you move away. If you were to use the **verb** *to welcome*, you might want to move toward the person or gesture them into your home. A good rule of thumb is that we move towards things we like – and things we're going after – and away from things we don't. This is especially true on stage. In auditions, it can be slight, but if you fully tempt someone in a moment, you may move toward them slightly, possibly by leaning forward in your chair or taking a small step forward. Obviously, you have to be careful that you don't move too much in auditions, as there is often a camera on you. In professional performances, however, your **intentions** will often lead you physically.

Again, specific **verbs** will often bring very interesting **behavior** out of you, but please don't think I'm telling you to flail your arms in a general way – that's never good. Explore the **physicality** verb choices can bring and don't censor your instincts.

Play Intentions, Not Results

Be aware that writers and directors who don't understand how actors work will give unhelpful notes and directions like *be angrier, be irritated, more sad, more embarrassed,* and so on (see the chapter on BAD DIRECTION). You must understand that attempting to play results like these will cause you to become inauthentic and play a faux feeling. It's best to change suggested results like these into strong **intentions** that are about the other actor and not about you. So if a director says, "I need more anger on that line," you might change your **intention** from *scold* to *castrate.* If you try to play the feeling or just get louder, the result is typically bad acting. Stay away from this result-oriented way of doing things whenever possible.

Verb-Scoring

I've included the following scene to illustrate how to **verb-score** material. It's not meant to be a phenomenal piece of writing, but simply to represent common auditioning dialogue. The **verbs** written here are just my ideas and are by no means the only possibilities. Remember, **verbs** represent the framework to play from, not a rigid, set-in-stone plan. You always want to be open to what the other actor gives you as well, as he or she will often play it completely differently than you thought they would. You may also work with a director who wants to take you in an entirely different direction. Do not be alarmed by this; expect it. It's all part of the creative process. I've scored both roles to show some possibilities for each. Typically you'll only score your own lines. I always recommend writing in pencil, as your choices will likely change throughout the process of working on a scene.

Stephanie quietly sneaks into the copy room while Whit's back is turned. She locks the door behind her.

flirt
                    STEPHANIE
          Hi, Whit.

                         WHIT   *greet*
          Hey, Stephanie, what's up?

bait
                    STEPHANIE
          Oh, I don't know. I thought that
          was really sweet what you did for
          me today.

                         WHIT   *deflect*
          No biggy. It's my job.

tantalize
                    STEPHANIE
          I just wanted to thank you
          personally.

She gets in his face.

                         WHIT   *reject*
          Whoa, Stephanie. I don't think
          that's such a good idea.

stimulate   STEPHANIE
          I like it.

decoy

> **WHIT**
> Maybe we could meet for a coffee later?

deflect

> **STEPHANIE**
> I don't want coffee.

She goes to undo his belt.

resist

> **WHIT**
> Stephanie, I don't know what you're trying to do, but I take my job seriously and if anyone comes in here—

reassure

> **STEPHANIE**
> I locked the door, Whit.

> **WHIT**
> You locked it?

implore

titillate

> **STEPHANIE**
> Yeah.

Her lips are really close to his now.

reason with

> **WHIT**
> What if someone hears us?

Flirty tease

> **STEPHANIE**
> Why would they hear us? Are you gonna make some noises?

humor/ evade

> **WHIT**
> Have you heard the joke about the guy who meets up with a bear, a squirrel and a llama?

reject

STEPHANIE

Not now, Whit.

WHIT

But it's *really* funny.   *plead*

dominate

STEPHANIE

I want you to take my clothes off
and make love to me on this copy
machine, okay?

                                            deny

WHIT

I don't think that's a good idea.

warn

STEPHANIE

Whit, I'm gonna give you about ten
seconds and if you don't have sex
with me, I'll tell everyone in this
office that you tried to take
advantage of me in the copy room
and you'll get fired. Is that what
you want?

WHIT   *tame*

You wouldn't.

toy with

STEPHANIE

Oh, yes I would, Whitty.

WHIT

You're evil.   *insult/rebuke*

tempt

STEPHANIE

Yes, I am. Do it, Whit.

                    WHIT   *nibble*
           This is crazy.

      arouse   STEPHANIE
           Just relax and enjoy yourself.

She moves in.

Even though I gave every line in this scene a **verb**, there's no rule that says you must. If you're anal about **verb-scoring** correctly, you'll likely fail. Sometimes an entire paragraph just needs one **verb**, and sometimes it needs four. Don't get stuck with trying to apply a rule here as it can be confusing and defeat the purpose.

Years ago when I was still acting, I had an audition to play a small part on a TV show. The first scene was just the one line, "Freeze! Don't move," and the stage direction read *with intensity.* I wanted to stand out from the rest, and this scene only gave me one line to do that. Since the type of gun wasn't specified, I first decided to mime a shotgun instead of a handgun, which is what I was pretty sure everyone else was going to do. Then I asked myself, "What **intention** can I use besides *to intimidate?*" I knew that every actor that came in to read for this part would scream the line and pull a finger-gun. I decided to bring a bit of lightness to the line and ended up using *to terrorize* on "Freeze," and then *to toy with* for "Don't move." So, in a line that seemingly only had one note, I brought two and booked the role. Production later confirmed it was because of my creative interpretation of that one line. I only tell you this story to illustrate my point and to help you to understand how **intentions** can literally get you the job.

Finding the Lightness

Talented actors tend to find the humor or lightness in their work. I don't mean to say that they just throw it in, but they look for where it could be. Even if it's a really dark break-up scene, they may laugh in the middle as if to say, "This is how it's gonna end, huh? Your gonna give me the 'It's not you, it's me' speech?"

If a scene is really heavy, there may room for some ironic lightness or even flirtation. There's always that villain who enjoys the power of it all – again, Heath Ledger's performance is a great example. Too many people miss this concept, so if you can find it, you'll stand out in the best of ways. Casting will think, "Wow, I never even saw it that way." Even if they don't, they'll typically give you credit for being creative enough to find it. Yes, there are some scenes that have nothing light about them, but if Nick Nolte can find it in *Affliction* – an extremely dark film – you can find it in your next audition. Watch Nolte bring humor to almost every scene in that movie. He understands that dark material like that needs lightness somewhere. Without it, the performance would come off much too heavy.

11

OBSTACLES

The emotional and physical blocks that your character must overcome to achieve his or her objective.

A friend of mine, who I consider to be an inspiration in my life, had massive **obstacles**. He came to Los Angeles to become an actor without knowing anyone. He hadn't even finished high school. When he got to LA, he had no job skills, no money, and no place to live. *Big* **obstacles**. Some of this may sound familiar to you if you took big risks by choosing to be an artist.

As fate would have it, he soon met people who were kind enough to let him sleep on their couch in exchange for helping to clean their apartment. He eventually got a job making minimum wage, but still struggled to keep it all together. Emotionally, he was in bad shape. He didn't think much of himself. His father used to beat him up pretty badly on a regular basis and verbally abused him, calling him dumb and telling him he'd never make it in life. Those words were so ingrained in my friend that he carried them wherever he went. I met him in Larry Moss' class, where he would often stay after class was over and rehearse late into the night, sometimes falling asleep there. His work in class was average. His fears and feelings about himself translated to vocal issues and other big problems on the stage. His spelling was so bad that he had serious trouble filling out checks and carried a pocket dictionary wherever he went. So, a list of his **obstacles** would look like this:

- Panic attacks

- No money

- Not knowing anyone in LA

- No job skills

- Physical and verbal abuse

- Low self-worth

- Spelling issues

- Vocal issues

- No agent

- No manager

- Mediocre talent

We eventually lost touch, but I heard that he booked a commercial and used the money to rent an apartment and join SAG. The next time I bumped into him several years later, he was twenty-eight and had just signed with his first agent. He was back in class and had noticeably improved. He was taking voice classes and was in therapy for his panic attacks. He had stopped speaking to his father and had made peace with the decision to do so. One day, I saw him in class and congratulated him on a small role he had booked. It was just a few lines, but it was his first part on a show and he was excited just like anyone would be. He later went on to book a lead in an award-winning TV show and is now a highly respected actor.

Christopher Reeve once said, "I think a hero is an ordinary individual who finds strength to persevere and endure in spite of overwhelming **obstacles**." I'm sure there were other **obstacles** my friend had to deal with that I never knew about, but despite all these roadblocks, he ascended and achieved. His is a hero's story. He did everything within his power to attain his **super-objective**, *to be a respected actor and prove my dad wrong.*

```
Obstacle (ăb • sti • kəl) n.
   something that impedes progress or achievement.
```

Merriam-Webster Dictionary

When you see a performance that rivets you, it is because the actor playing the part is absolutely determined to overcome the **obstacles**. Michael Jordan said, "If you're trying to achieve something, you'll hit road blocks. I've had them; everyone has had them. But **obstacles** don't have to stop you. If you run into a wall, don't turn around and give up; figure out how to climb it, go through it, or work around it". All great characters work to rise above all emotional, physical, and mental blocks on the way to their **super-objectives**.

How far would you go to accomplish your **super-objective**? What **obstacles** do you want to obliterate? As an actor, it's important to identify the **obstacles** that stand in your character's way. Doing so will deepen your performance, clarify for you what the character has to overcome, and make it that much more satisfying to achieve your **super-objective**. Some of these **obstacles** will be very apparent from the **given circumstances** after having done the homework. Others must be assumed and invented by you, which will further raise the **stakes**. After all, it's much more interesting to watch someone struggle against big **obstacles** than to watch them have no trouble at all. Yes, sometimes what's standing in your way will be small, but other times it will be a mountain. It's your job to know the difference.

Remember that movie I did on a glacier? It was the true story of a rugby team that crash-landed in the Andes Mountains and had to survive there for nearly three months. The **obstacles** of that story are what make it compelling and exciting. If the characters had had enough food, a comfortable place to stay, and knew perfectly well how to return home without any trouble, it would've been a very boring movie. Instead, they ran out of food and were forced to eat the bodies of their teammates who didn't survive. Not only are the **stakes** high, but the **obstacles** are huge. Can you imagine having to eat a friend to survive? And remember, it's a true story! So, let's look at what my character's **obstacles** were:

- The wind chill sent the temperature down to $-20^{\circ}F$ at times.
- The food ran out.
- Drinking water easily froze.
- Some teammates were lying about food. I didn't know whom to trust.
- Feelings of loneliness and despair.
- Fear of avalanches.
- Fear of freezing to death.
- The emotional strain of having lost half of the team in the crash.

Forgetting how any of these **obstacles** affected my character would've taken the audience out of the reality of the film. The struggle is what that story was all about. Oh, and there were **obstacles** in the actual filming process as well. This was one of those rare movies that was shot largely in sequence because they had to show us becoming thinner and thinner from the lack of food. I lost thirty pounds, taking me down to 140, which, at 5'10", wasn't a healthy look for me. There were also twenty other young actors in the cast, all with very different personalities and egos that would sometimes clash.

Sometimes the weather even proved itself to be one of the most dangerous **obstacles**. One day, after shooting on the glacier, a few of us boarded a helicopter to be flown back to the town we were staying in. There was a complete whiteout, which meant zero visibility. The pilot looked panicked as he fought with the controls and tried to establish where the mountain was so we didn't crash into it. The chopper kept making strange noises and dropping ten feet at a time without warning. Thankfully, the pilot navigated us back to safety and we all lived to tell the tale.

Midnight Cowboy

In the film *Midnight Cowboy,* starring Jon Voight and Dustin Hoffman, both characters struggle against significant **obstacles**. Voight's character, Joe Buck, moves to New York to achieve his **super-objective**, *to be a rich, male prostitute*. He has an emotional hang-up from being gang-raped, he's much too nice and trusting for New York, and he has to deal with the fear involved with moving from a small town to a big city. Voight played Buck's naïveté beautifully, standing around looking at the buildings in wide-eyed wonder. Eventually he faces more **obstacles**: he runs out of money and no one will pay him for sex. He finally sleeps with an older woman, thinking he'll be paid, but she becomes an **obstacle**, too, when she cries and becomes angry that he would ask her to pay. He has no friends – another **obstacle** – until he meets Ratso, who lies and steals his money, thereby becoming another **obstacle** for Buck. They eventually team up, but have nowhere to sleep until they find an empty, abandoned building. Unfortunately, it's too cold there to sleep – another **obstacle** – and they get kicked out. All of these **obstacles** were part of the **given circumstances** for Voight.

Hoffman's character, Ratso Rizzo, dreams of escaping New York and being warm and happy in Florida. He has to deal with the **obstacles** of walking with a limp, having no friends besides Joe, being terminally ill with a sickness that makes him cough more and more violently as the film progresses, living in a dilapidated building with no heat and no money, having insecurities about his physical challenges, and feeling the fear of dying alone.

As you can see, this script is filled with great **obstacles** that, for the most part, keep the characters in constant struggle. Even though neither of them fully achieves his **super-objective** they do their best to deal with and overcome their **obstacles**. Identify your character's **obstacles** and your performance will be layered and full.

All in all, **identifying obstacles allows you to be clear about what your character is fighting against**, which creates compelling story-telling. They help to create real character depth, not faux character depth.

Obstacles in Auditions

Sometimes you won't have the benefit of being able to read an entire script before an audition. Usually, you just receive a few scenes and a character description. If the **obstacles** aren't apparent, you'll have to invent them based on the small amount of information you have. Let's say you're reading for a character whose **objective** is *to get you to go out on a date with me*, but you can see from the dialogue that he's having a difficult time getting the words out. If there are no clear **obstacles**, you must figure them out through your detective work or invent them. People who are shy around romantic interests typically have emotional issues like, *I'm not attractive enough, I'm not experienced enough,* or *they're going to use me for money or sex.* If you assume that your character has struck out before, you may invent an experience where your character was laughed at and shamed by a love interest. I really want to emphasize the point that inventing **obstacles** is essential when you don't know what your character is fighting against. Otherwise, you'll end up indicating the feelings and weakening your performance.

Personalizing Obstacles

When your character's **obstacles** are difficult to connect to –
because you haven't struggled with them personally or because you
feel resolved about those particular issues in your life – using
substitution for your **obstacles** can be an effective choice. Let's say
you had a character with that same **objective** – *to get you to hire me* –
and it was in the **given circumstances** that your character doesn't
think he or she is smart. If you know you're intelligent, connecting to
the character through that specific **obstacle** will be very difficult. So
to personalize it, you might think of one of your own personal
obstacles. Maybe you're embarrassed about your father or the fact
that you've never worked as an actor. Using your **real life**,
imagination, or a **50/50**, you could then come up with a **trigger** that
brings out that insecurity. You could also give yourself the **as if** that
the character you're about to talk to just heard about your father or
your lack of career. Doing so would help you connect and understand
the character's **obstacle**, so you don't have to indicate the struggle,
but really have a secret one. Once you have that, you can go after
your **objective**.

12

PHYSICAL BEHAVIOR

The physical choices that reveal the inner workings of your character.

My grandfather was a merchant by trade and was very particular in the way he conducted his business. His **behavior** was always very precise, whether in bookkeeping, the use of the cash register, or even counting out change for a customer. His physical business and how it related to who he was and what he did was never more apparent to me than when he made himself breakfast. It was his favorite meal of the day and I would often wake up early when I visited him just to watch the show. His **behavior** was meticulous, specific and never changed a bit until the day he died. He liked his eggs poached medium-well. Never over-cooked. To ensure the perfect product, he would often stand over them like a hawk and pat them with his index finger while carrying on a conversation with me.

When the eggs were done, he would take the metal egg holders to the table and use a butter knife to scrape the eggs onto his plate. Since he had also been a child of the Great Depression and never wanted to waste a bit of his precious meal, he would continue to scrape until every last bit of egg was there, like a miner searching for gold. He would then put his bread in the toaster and would always double-check that the dial was on the right setting to brown his toast exactly how he liked it. Because the toaster was old, it sometimes produced over-done toast, so he would scrape off the burned bits in the sink. Then he would butter his toast with the precision of a surgeon, always making sure he had the perfect amount.

The salt and pepper were my personal favorites. He would first hold the salt shaker over his plate with his right hand, and pat the back of his hand with his left as he carefully distributed the salt over the eggs. He would then put a bit of pepper into his left hand and, balling his hand into a fist, sprinkle it around the eggs, squeezing his hand like a peppermill. Every bite would receive twenty chews before being swallowed. I counted.

This **behavior** spoke volumes about who my grandfather was. Not only was he precise in his bookkeeping, but in every aspect of his life. He grew up on a farm, where his breakfast came straight from the few chickens they had in their barn. As an actor, I actually stole his salt and pepper routine for a methodic villain I played and for years, people would ask me about that one moment in the film.

In life, as in acting, what a person does often speaks exponentially louder than what they say, especially if they're not always truthful. I cannot stress the importance of **behavior** enough. When actors neglect it, performances risk falling flat. When they employ it creatively, we witness something amazingly real. When coming up with your characters' **behavior**, make sure to consider the **given circumstances** – especially their occupation, flaws, and location – as well as their **objectives** and emotional life.

I worked with a young actor whose career had stalled after ten years of consistent work in film and television. When it came time to do her first scene in class from Kenneth Lonergan's *This is Our Youth*, she walked in with her partner and sat on the couch, stiffly delivering lines. After a minute or so I realized that she was stuck there without any real **behavior** and I stopped the scene.

MICHAEL: Let's talk about this much.

BETH: Thank you! I feel horrible up here.

MICHAEL: First off, welcome back to the stage. It's been a while, so I know you're nervous.

BETH: Thanks, it's still really awkward.

MICHAEL: Do you know why you feel awkward?

BETH: Not really, I just don't know what to do with myself.

MICHAEL: Well, on some level, that's perfect. She likes him, she's alone for the first time with a guy she really has a crush on.

BETH: Right.

MICHAEL: But you're not doing anything. You need **behavior**.

BETH: But it's not my place.

MICHAEL: No, but you have yourself. You have your purse.

BETH: Yeah.

MICHAEL: Ever been in a situation like this?

BETH: Yeah.

MICHAEL: Great. Do you remember what your awkward feelings caused you to do physically?

BETH: I dunno… sometimes when I get nervous I play with my hair.

MICHAEL: That could be interesting. What else? What do you do when you get insecure around a guy you like?

BETH: Well… I'm usually worried that my lipstick's smudged or that I've put on too much make-up.

MICHAEL: Great, that's perfect. So, let's start there. Start the scene again, and I want you to try that choice with your hair, that thing you do, and do you have a compact with you?

BETH: Yeah.

MICHAEL: You have any tissue or anything?

BETH: Yeah.

MICHAEL: Perfect, so I want you to use the compact to check your make-up and use a tissue to remove some. Try that.

They began again, and it was much better than the first attempt.

MICHAEL: Okay, great, how'd that feel?

BETH: So much better.

MICHAEL: Yeah, it was much better, because you had real **behavior** that you do when you feel nervous around someone. And the make-up thing is perfect because this girl is very fashion-oriented, and if she knows about fashion, it's reasonable to say that she knows about make-up. Okay, now the next thing. You're sitting on the couch.

BETH: Yeah.

MICHAEL: How do you feel about him?

BETH: I like him but I've been burned before.

MICHAEL: Right. Why else would she react like that to his joke about locking the door at the beginning? That's a hint the writer's given you.

BETH: Yeah.

MICHAEL: What's your **objective**?

BETH: Well, I might want to make out, but I want him to respect me first. And I want to make sure he's not going to use me.

MICHAEL: Can you state that in a simple way?

BETH: I'm not just some slut that he can have his way with.

MICHAEL: Great. So the couch... kind of make-out territory, right?

BETH: Yeah.

MICHAEL: You okay with being there so soon?

BETH: No.

MICHAEL: Right. So, do you see how your actions aren't lining up with the character's **needs**? If you want to be respected first before anything like that happens, you can't sit on the couch. No matter what a character says, what they do speaks louder.

BETH: Right.

MICHAEL: So, you may want to stand a bit longer or sit in that chair over there before going to the couch. Now, as the scene progresses, do you think it's possible that you guys might kiss?

BETH: Maybe.

MICHAEL: So what about breath mints or gum? You have any in your purse?

BETH: Yeah, gum.

MICHAEL: Okay, so after you finish your make-up, I want you to think, "He might kiss me," and go for a piece of gum. Let's try it again.

The scene became fuller and even more believable and the actress never entered another scene without **behavior**.

Occupation

Peoples' occupations spawn countless doings. Ambitious corporate types can often be seen checking their smartphones, returning emails, doing a crossword, and reading the paper all while drinking their coffee. The occupations people choose often say a lot about them, and so being creative with **behavior** based on that one piece of information can be extremely effective.

Let's take the simple idea of having breakfast. If you're playing an actor, you might read a script and highlight your lines, smoke a cigarette, call your agent, or text a friend. You could read the cereal box, dig around in it for the toy, or eat straight out of it because you have no money for milk. Maybe you mouth the lines to an audition scene or cram down a health bar while doing your make-up. A hooker might spray perfume onto her cleavage, count her money from the previous night, flirt with a patron, put on lipstick, take off make-up, cover up a bruise, pull up her stockings, lick the cream out of a Danish, or do coke from a spoon. If you're playing someone who doesn't have a job, you could look through the classifieds, eat a bread roll with a glass of water because that's all you can afford, or steal the condiments off the table of a diner.

Never forget that peoples' careers greatly affect their **behavior** both in real life and in scripts. Determine your character's occupation, find real people to observe, and be creative with your **physical behavior**.

Objective

People who actively go after what they want do so not only verbally, but physically as well. If your character's **objective** is *to get you to want me*, your audience should be able to see it in your actions. You might show up with a gift, use breath spray, reveal part of your body, eat something sexy like a juicy strawberry, stroke a wine glass, touch your partner's hair or leg, or make a perfect cocktail for the object of your desire. If you're going after *to get you to confess,* and your character is one to use intimidation, you might sharpen a knife, play with or clean a gun, smoke a cigar, do a drug, smash or break things, build a bomb, or cut up and eat a bloody steak. Always consider how a character's **objective** might inform his **physical behavior**.

Flaws

All great characters have flaws, and all great flaws influence **behavior**. In *As Good as It Gets*, Jack Nicholson displays his character's OCD in numerous and brilliant ways. He brings his own plastic utensils to a diner where he always sits at the same table, orders the same thing and requires the same waitress. Before arriving home – where he locks and unlocks his door and turns his lights on and off five times each – he avoids every crack on the sidewalk. When putting on his slippers, he taps the floor on either side with the appropriate foot. Washing his hands requires multiple fresh bars of soap. All the various ways in which we get to see his OCD are wonderful, and while some of them were likely written into the script, I am certain that Nicholson found others on his own. Either way, you can see how **behavior** based on a single trait made his performance multi-layered and engaging to watch.

Emotional Life

The way we go about **physical behavior** is often based on how we are feeling at the time. Let's say you're having a fight with your roommate. If you're in the middle of cutting vegetables while arguing, the energy of the fight will transfer into the way you handle the knife. If you find out your lover is cheating on you and want to get the hell out of the apartment, you probably wouldn't neatly and calmly pack your clothes in a bag. You're more likely to cram them in there with an anger-driven velocity. Likewise, if your dog just passed away, it would look ridiculous if you playfully vacuumed your apartment. Always remember that emotions and circumstances greatly affect how people do what they do.

A Common Mistake

I often have to remind less-experienced actors to speak through their **physical behavior**. They sometimes have the tendency to stop what they're doing, deliver a line, and then resume their activity. In real life, we tend to continue our cooking, cleaning, organizing, dressing, etc., while talking. This is not a rigid rule, however. If we really want to make a point, we may stop our action for a moment to do so, but then we get back to the task at hand. Use your instincts, but favor the side of continuing your activities.

As important and dynamic as this element of the technique can be, most of the time you must be careful not to make your **behavior** the focus of a scene. If your activities keep you from listening and responding to your partner, you'll risk losing your audience.

13

DESTINATION

Moving with purpose.

In life, people don't just get up and go places for no reason. Every decision we make on a daily basis to move from here to there is based on very specific needs under very particular circumstances. Look at the actions you take in a day. You get up from the couch to go to the fridge because you're hungry. Then you need to check your emails, so you go to the computer. You remember that it's your best friend's birthday and you go to find your phone to call him. You and your friend make plans to meet up for lunch so you go to the closet to put on your coat and then find your keys. It goes on and on. Life is filled with **destinations** that are based on peoples' needs and circumstances. Your work as an actor should be no different.

Every good director and acting coach knows about **destination**. Movement in scenes is almost always better than two people just sitting on a couch, and it must always be justified. Some less-experienced actors stand up from the couch or take three steps to the left for no reason, and while their actor's instinct to move might feel justified, it's often just a need to move out of nervousness or insecurity and reads to the audience as such. Sometimes a script or a director will tell you to go to a table or a desk on a certain line, in which case you must do your best to justify the movement. Always give yourself a reason to go somewhere, and if you can't, just stay where you are. Other times, scripts won't have any movement in the stage direction. In this case, it's left up to you to find your own **destinations** and to justify them.

Remember that **destination** is powerful not only because it makes performances more truthful, but also because it will make you more comfortable, less nervous, and clearer about what you are doing. I realize that you don't always have the freedom to go where you want while on a set, but if a director gives you the freedom, make the most of it and follow your impulse to move. Don't short-change your performances. Neglecting **destination** contradicts what we do in real life. You must always know where you're going and why.

14

ENVIRONMENT

*How does the place affect your character
emotionally and physically?*

Lights come up on a shabby, one-room apartment in Manhattan. A sofa bed sits on stage with grimy sheets and dirty pillows. A beat up old clock sits on the floor, surrounded by trash. Empty food cans are scattered around the place. Hanging over the window is a soiled and tattered blanket. In the corner sits a man in his early twenties. Using a can opener, he punches a hole in a can of condensed milk. He drinks its contents, then removes the lid and scrapes the rest out with his fingers.

This is how Alan Bowne's play *Beirut* begins. It takes place in a possible future where an unnamed, highly contagious disease has killed millions and all the sick are quarantined to live in abandoned buildings. The man on stage, Torch, is among them. This play is about sickness, and if it's built correctly, the audience will be able to tell just by seeing the place the character lives in. Torch lives quite like an animal in an unkempt cage. "Where you are is who you are," Stella Adler once said. This is what she meant.

If you're playing Torch, you must understand that this is your character's life. This is what you're stuck in. It's **as if** you're a diseased, dying animal in a cage. There's nothing comfortable about it and that's the writer's intention. If you start the scene with neat, clean hair and a nice, ironed polo shirt, you've missed the hint from the stage directions about the place; there is no shower and there is no comb. This is what the **given circumstances** tell you. As the actor, the hints given to you by the **environment** about the life and world of the character must affect your emotions and **behavior**.

Ever notice how you feel at a black tie event versus how you feel at the beach? How does your **behavior** change from one place to the next? At the dinner party, you may feel inferior because your pants are ten years old and also happen to be highwaters. Perhaps your shirt has a stain on it. You may look at the appetizers and wonder if that table of food cost more than your car. Maybe you steal a few sandwiches for later. On the beach, maybe you're proud of your toned body, so you take your shirt off, put on some tanning oil, then prop yourself up perfectly for everyone to see. However, your best friend feels far more comfortable at the dinner party because he has the most expensive suit there, but at the beach he feels fat, so he covers his stomach with a towel. If you're playing a character in these **environments**, you have to consider whether this **environment** makes him feel comfortable or not, and what **behavior** comes out of that feeling.

When my mom was a little kid, her family was very poor so she had never been to a fancy restaurant. One day, some friends invited her family out to the nicest place in town. My mom, just eight years old, had no idea how to behave in a place like that, so she watched the other patrons and copied what she saw. She picked up her fork and knife to cut her food the way a woman nearby had just done. She noticed a napkin on someone's lap and hurriedly placed hers on her own. Apparently, the man sitting at the next table was quite thirsty, because he picked up his water glass and drank it all in one go. So my mom did the same thing; she thought it was polite. Then the waiter came around and filled her glass again. Thinking it was the right thing to do, she downed it all as quickly as she could. Once more the refill, once more the drinking. By the fourth refill, her mother could tell by the look on my mom's young face that something was wrong. "Mom, they refilled it again," she said with puppy-dog eyes. "You don't have to drink it, honey." My mom was so relieved. How was she supposed to know? Sometimes characters feel completely at home in their surroundings; sometimes the feel totally out of place and need to compensate as a result.

Hot & Cold

Earlier we talked about incorporating weather into your **moment before**, dealing with all types of conditions in the first few moments of a scene. Sometimes, however, you'll have to deal with temperature *during* a scene and there are very specific things to consider.

Let's first talk about what to do when you're working on material wherein the climate is hot. First, where do they most noticeably sweat? Perhaps they sweat on their upper lip, lower back, armpits, or forehead. Next, figure out how they might ease that discomfort. What might they use to wipe off the sweat? Perhaps they would use the back of their hand or their shirt. If they're upper class, maybe a handkerchief. Also, be sure to consider where the sun is in the sky. The effect of a noontime sun is much different than that of a morning or evening sun. Would they wear a hat? Is it a dry heat or a humid heat? How do they try to cool down? Do they fan themselves with something? Does their speech slow down? Maybe they pull their shirt away from the areas that feel hottest. I once saw a man put his hat in a sprinkler and then put it back on his head. Keep in mind that when people are hot, their movements tend to slow down.

Part of the play *Hooters,* by Ted Tally, takes place on the beach. I saw a wonderful production here in LA where a section of the set was covered in sand. There were moments where they had to cross from one side of the stage to the other, and the first time it happened, I saw the character come to the realization *as he was walking* that the sand was burning hot, so he made the rest of his journey **as if** he was walking on hot coals. The audience screamed with laughter every time he crossed. The actors also turned their chairs according to where the sun was in the sky, which created great believability. This is a clear example of how actors can use the place to affect their **behavior**.

The same technique applies for low temperatures. Consider where your character is cold, and how she gets warm. As the character, do you pull up your collar to ease the biting wind on the back of your neck? Do you rub the back of your arms to warm them up? If there's a heavy wind, which direction is it coming from? Perhaps you turn your back on it in order to shield your face. Also, when people are cold, their movements tend to be more brisk.

Hot or cold, consider all of the effects of temperature, as well as the **behavior** that you exhibit as a result. You may even explore your own personal **behavior** when you're hot or cold and bring it to your work. You don't always need to believe or feel the cold yourself, because your actions will cause the audience to believe it. The important part is that the sensory elements are present without being a distraction from the scene.

Fourth wall

I often tell my clients, "Give yourself a **fourth wall** that helps you." The **fourth wall** is the term given to what you see when you look toward the audience or – in some film and television situations – in the direction of the camera. For on-camera work, the term can also apply to a blue/green screen where scenery or a computer-generated image will be added in later. Production might mark your focus point for a huge tree or terrifying monster with a piece of tape, but you have to imagine what the character sees. When the actor playing Torch in *Beirut* looks toward the audience, he could imagine a dirty, peeling wall with boarded-up windows. In addition to all of the other work he must do, this choice could serve as emotional fuel for the actor, heightening his feeling of being trapped.

The **fourth wall** also encloses the space you're working in and establishes a sense of privacy and intimacy for you on the set or stage. When you do the work of building the **fourth wall**, the audience will feel like they're witnessing something real rather than being performed to. It's particularly important when you're working on sexual or highly emotional scenes where a sense of privacy will help you to be brave and feel free.

Let's look at the *Hooters* scene again. If the two actors were to look in the direction of the audience without building a **fourth wall** for themselves, they might become self-conscious. Seeing people in their seats is not going to help them feel like they're at the beach. A much more effective approach is to create the entire beach in their minds' eye, complete with rolling waves and groups of people nearby – maybe some cute girls. The actors will feel a sense of privacy and the audience will be drawn in even more.

If you see people in front of you, or a camera in your face, you might give a self-conscious performance or do what many actors do, which is to ignore that direction entirely. If there were an actual wall there or just scenery, you would naturally look there once in a while. Just don't look directly into the camera or at audience members unless directed to do so.

Let's look at one more example with the play *Proof* by David Auburn. Catherine's father has just died in the house where she lived with him for most of her life and the entire play takes place on the back porch. If, as Catherine, you were to avoid the **fourth wall** and not look out into your backyard, it would be very distracting to the audience. Building the backyard is hugely important for them *and* for you. It's yours to create, and I believe that in this case, it should be tied to the father. There are **triggers** throughout the play and it doesn't hurt to put some memories of your father out there. You could see a swing set your father used to push you on when you were a kid, the tree house he built for you, or maybe an apple tree that you would pick together. All of these examples provide you with the possible **triggering** thought, *I'll never get to do that with him again.*

Some actors I work with find it helpful to draw a picture of the **fourth wall**. Whatever you decide, build one that is personal and emotionally full for you. Create it so that it enriches your performance.

Don't expect to see your whole imagined wall at any given moment. Most often, you'll see one thing at a time – a picture, a mirror, a fireplace, a cute girl or guy flirting with you, etc. It can be helpful to give yourself focus points, such as placing the flirtatious person where a lighting stand is on the set. The sound booth in the back of the theatre could be where your old tree house sits. The exit sign could become the moon or a star. If you're working with a blue/green screen, the director may give you a focus point, and if not, ask for one.

Note: Never look directly into the camera or acknowledge people in the audience unless the material is written that way or you're directed to do so.

Personalizing the Place

Some actors feel more connected when they give themselves a place from their own lives that carries the same emotional charge as the one in the script. This can be extremely effective. If you're working on the role of Catherine in *Proof*, you might look out into the **fourth wall** and picture your grandparent's backyard. If you were close to your grandfather and you lost him, this might be a very emotional choice for you. As long as it helps the scene and doesn't take you away from your partner, it will be powerful.

Let's say you're working on a scene involving a break-up and, in your **real life**, you actually had a terrible break-up at a restaurant. See what it's like doing the scene **as if** you were back in that restaurant. Perhaps you have a scene where you're supposed to be sexy and free. You could envision your own bedroom, or some other area where you've felt extremely comfortable in that way.

Whether you build it from the script or make it up from scratch, **environment** can provide you with lots of hints about how to play the character and embody authentic **behavior**. So, you must ask yourself where the scene takes place, how it makes your character feel, and what kind of **behavior** arises because of those feelings. Walking over the sand in *Hooters*, drinking condensed milk out of a can in *Beirut*, and mimicking people at an upscale restaurant the way my mom did as a child are all perfect examples of how **behavior** is influenced by **environment** and how the person feels in it.

15

CHARACTER WORK

The building blocks for creating a character.

I think about how accessible information is online these days and I feel more than ever that there are no excuses for failing to do the work. As an actor in scene study class, one of my first experiences with **character work** was playing the role of Rudy in Martin Sherman's play, *Bent*. The character was a challenging role for me since it was so far from who I am. I was excited to jump in and tackle it. Rudy is written as a homosexual dancer working in Berlin during the Nazi occupation. During Hitler's reign, being gay was not just illegal; it was considered sub-human. They were persecuted as horribly, if not more so, than Jews and criminals. This kind of discrimination was something I didn't understand.

My first task was to find documentaries, pictures and stories from that time. The research I did affected me greatly. I also visited the Museum of Tolerance where, during the last segment of the tour, I sat in a reconstructed gas chamber. I imagined being forced in there with friends and strangers to spend my final moments. Relating to the absolute horror of what all these people went through made me weep.

Now that I had educated myself more thoroughly on World War II, I met with my scene partner – who played Max – to talk about **super-objectives**. I chose *to survive and be loved*. Next, I was ready to explore physical choices. I knew I wanted the character to come off feminine both physically and verbally. Rudy's boyfriend, Max, is written as a very masculine guy, so in addition to the vulnerability the femininity would bring me, it provided a contrast to Max. I asked my coach at the time if there were any performances for me to watch and he suggested William Hurt in *Kiss of the Spiderwoman*. I was inspired greatly by Hurt's drastic transformation. I loved his use of long breaths and his way of speaking. I also knew I wanted to incorporate the humanity and sense of humor that Michael Jeter brought to his role as the homeless cabaret singer in one of my favorite films of all time, *The Fisher King*.

I started exploring Rudy's posture and determined that leading from my pelvis, in addition to giving myself the feeling that my joints were extra oiled, hooked me in the most. I began to feel very loose physically, free like a dancer, and more open. I then thought I should pick an animal that represented Rudy both physically and energetically and decided on the peacock. I visited the zoo to study the animal and started to incorporate the feeling of the peacock's open chest. Wardrobe was next, and I had to be careful not to choose anything that would detract from the character. He couldn't exactly look like he was gay because of the time, and I was sure he would be used to hiding it. So, I found an accessory – a very subtle scarf – that would make him feel pretty. Next were his glasses. I had an old pair of my grandfather's from the forties that were perfect. Once I had the lenses changed out, I was ready to rehearse.

My scene partner and I decided, since our scene took place in the woods, that we would meet up and run it in Griffith Park as it would help us with **environment** and create our **fourth wall** for us. After rehearsal, I knew I needed to go back and do some work. I poured more time into my backstory and my **relationship** to Max and felt even more solid. But there was still one thing I was struggling with. I felt uncomfortable with my character's sexual preference. Not being gay and trying to be convincingly intimate with another man was difficult for me to wrap my head around. I wasn't attracted to my scene partner the way Rudy was attracted to Max, so I decided to find something beautiful about my partner to focus on. The guy I was working with had really great eyes, so I went with that. Throughout the next rehearsal, I focused on his eyes and the **emotional relationship** I had created. To connect myself with him even more, I imagined that he had struggled with some of the same childhood issues as I had (see the section on *Shared Events* in the EMOTIONAL TRIGGERS chapter) and I instantly felt more love for him.

After two weeks of working on the scene, we put it up in class, which turned out to be very rewarding. Playing someone who was so different from me but not as much as I had once thought still stands out as being one of the greatest artistic experiences of my life.

The rest of this chapter is dedicated to breaking down and highlighting the important elements of **character work** that are required with the rest of the technique. Remember, 'character' means *a flesh and blood human being – or other life form – that is believable.* If the audience can see the work, it's no good. If your portrayal of the character isn't truthful and the work you do is just an excuse for you to show off, you're missing the point. Rehearsing on your own or with a scene partner isn't just about blocking or running lines. It's about immersing yourself into the life of your character and exploring choices.

Never Judge Your Character & Worldview

A client came to me to work on an audition for a role in a wonderful film. The minute she walked in the door, she said, "Okay, this girl is a bitch. I absolutely hate her." When I asked if there was *anything* she liked about her, she said, "No one could find anything to like about this girl." The judgment she had about this character would make it impossible for her to play her convincingly, so we sat down to begin reading so I could help her find compassion for her character.

MICHAEL: Why is the character like this?

JODIE: No reason that I can see.

MICHAEL: Okay, then why does she hate her mother?

JODIE: Because her mother is poor and victimy and she wants to break away from her and be rich and famous.

MICHAEL: Okay, good. Let's focus on the fact that she's poor. Have you ever been poor?

JODIE: Yeah, right now. I can barely afford this coaching.

MICHAEL: And how do you feel about that?

JODIE: Angry sometimes. I want more.

MICHAEL: Great. Do you feel the distance between you and the character getting smaller already?

JODIE: Yeah, I guess. A little.

MICHAEL: Have you ever been terrified that you might not have enough to eat?

JODIE: No, it's never been that bad.

MICHAEL: How would you feel if it got that bad?

JODIE: Scared and angry?

MICHAEL: Angry enough to never want to go through that again? Angry enough to take it out on the person that's supposed to take care of you?

JODIE: Yeah, I'd want to get the hell out.

MICHAEL: Right, now you're in the world of the character. You feel resentment toward your mom. Why can't she stop being so weak and protect you? Why do you have to do all the planning for the both of you?

JODIE: Okay, yeah. I get it now.

MICHAEL: She's so scared and angry that she'd do almost anything to keep from feeling weak. So now that you understand her, let's go to the technique and work on it. You can never judge your character. You have to understand her and find out what pain lies under her actions. Only then can you play a real person. Get it?

JODIE: Yeah, I get it.

MICHAEL: Okay, let's work.

This is a straightforward example of an actor judging a character. It's very difficult to play someone you don't have empathy or sympathy for. Always look for the reason behind the **behavior**. Although some characters may judge themselves harshly, most don't think what they're doing is bad or wrong in any way. They justify their **behavior**, so you must as well. Rather than creating distance between you and your character, look instead to find a connection.

An exercise that can be helpful in understanding your character is to come up with a **worldview** based upon the **given circumstances**. Sometimes the text makes the **worldview** clear and sometimes you have to derive it through your detective work. Look at the character's history, how he is treated by others, how he reacts to that treatment, what he says and –often most importantly – what he does. All this information will tell you how the character views the world, which is best phrased in the following way:

• My name is (character's name), and the world is (six descriptive words or phrases).

For example, after watching Daniel Day-Lewis' performance in *There Will Be Blood*, it would be reasonable to say that after getting to know the text fully, Day-Lewis might have come up with something like, "My name is Daniel Plainview, and the world is filled with lying, betraying, greedy people that I must dominate and destroy before they trick me and take what is mine."

You want to walk into every performance with that kind of specificity about who you are and how you live in the world. Doing so creates more clarity in your performance so that if you end up losing sight of how your character might react in a situation, you can quickly get back into it by reminding yourself of your **worldview**.

Playing a Killer

Imagine that you're a dog with an abusive owner. After awhile, it would be safe to assume that you'd probably feel justified in biting or attacking anyone that provoked or threatened you, even if the person isn't your owner. This would make you like most killers, who are really victims that ultimately perpetuate violence.

Playing a villain can be tricky. As I mentioned earlier, avoid judgment and look to understand the reasons behind your character's actions. Villains have often been abused or mistreated in some way, whether it's included in the story or not. When they take their anger out on someone, they usually see the person who abused them. Consider the following quote from Denzel Washington: *"As an actor you have to be willing to play good and evil. Evil does exist and you have to be able to show it... I don't believe people are born evil. I believe evil takes over a person's soul because there are events in childhood or circumstances in life that can rob people of their dignity, rob people of hope, and turn them onto the wrong things in life."* Human beings need love, and if they are abused instead, that's what they give back to the world much of the time.

That being the case, killers – as well as other villains who don't actually kill – often don't feel remorse for their actions. Rather, they feel pleasure. In the same way the dog would feel vindicated in biting his abusive owner, the killer feels pleasure in hurting other people.

If you play a killer, it's important that you not only justify the act(s), but that you build the background of your own abuse in detail. Doing so will give you a clearer understanding of your character's psychology and will help you to further justify the act. Building at least three acts of background violence toward your character can be an extremely effective way to do this. Imagine the horrible events your character went through. This work, if done fully and specifically, should make you very sad as well as very angry. Again, doing this work intellectually won't serve your performance. *You must feel it.* If you have problems with this, I suggest that you pass on these roles. I have clients who look at some parts and say, "I don't want to subject myself to this." That's your choice, but if you're going to do it, do it right and seek to play a multi-dimensional character, not a cliché.

Oftentimes, there will be an element of sexual dominance in a male killer. This is because it's one of the most shaming forms of abuse he can inflict on another person. It's usually more about power than it is about sex. Again, these characters seek some kind of revenge on the people who abused them. Dominating a victim is their sick way of taking their sense of power back.

If you decide to take the route of using your imagination or a 50/50, ask yourself, "What event could happen in my life that would connect me to the emotional life of the character?" The answer to this question must also be strong enough to justify your actions and launch you into physically attacking someone, so be brave. A simple choice, such as, *This person raped my mother*, could be enough, as long as you fully visualize the event.

If you have difficulties building all the visuals with your imagination, or if you usually prefer to use more of your **real life** in your work, you may want to explore some of these **as ifs**. Before I share them with you, however, let me caution you. This can be very powerful stuff. You must be safe while using these choices. If, for any reason, a choice takes you into an out-of-control rage, it means you're not ready to use it. It's not acceptable to use people to act out any repressed anger. Be safe and be conscious of when a choice takes you out of control. Hurting yourself or someone else is not okay. That being said, here are the **as ifs**:

While committing violence on another character…

- Imagine that this person is responsible for a great pain you've struggled with your whole life.

- Imagine that this person caused your most difficult break-up.

- Imagine that this person committed a rape or an act of violence on a family member whom you're protective of.

- Imagine that this person is responsible for a death from your past.

- Imagine that this person is responsible for a horrible event you went through.

- Imagine that this person is responsible for a loved one's addiction, or that this person is the embodiment of the addiction itself.

- Imagine that this person is responsible for your parents' divorce.

- Imagine that this person is someone from your life who wronged you in some way.

- Imagine that this person is the embodiment of a disease that a loved one has or is struggling with.

To reiterate, always remember to seek to understand your character's actions and be safe and respectful towards yourself and other actors. As usual, if you're having trouble releasing the negative thoughts or feelings, see the section on *Letting the Feeling Go* in the EMOTIONAL TRIGGERS chapter.

Inside Out or Outside In

Building a character from the inside out means establishing your emotional connection by doing the foundational work of the technique before working on your **physicality**. Some people prefer this method while others work better when they find the character's wardrobe, voice and **physicality** before working emotionally. I heard that Hillary Swank didn't fully understand Brandon, her character in *Boys Don't Cry,* until she walked around Hollywood dressed *as a boy*. Walking around that way not only made her move differently, but she also began to experience first-hand how people treat cross-dressers. This likely gave Swank a strong impression of the shame that Brandon dealt with on a daily basis. This physical work was just the springboard she needed to understand and connect to the internal work of the life she was playing.

Years ago, a friend of mine was going out for the role of a politician's daughter in an Oliver Stone film. Casting was working quickly in choosing the right actor for this part, so she didn't have much time to prepare for the first audition. She recognized that the character's energy was quite different from her own and decided that her own daily wardrobe – mostly sundresses – was not going to help her. So, she went to the department store and found the perfect outfit: a pantsuit. She told me that simply putting it on immediately made her walk and feel differently. After her audition, Stone was so impressed that he gave her a callback and eventually – after she had the chance to do the internal work – booked her for the job. This is a great example of how working from the outside in can be extremely effective. Many of my female clients swear that just finding the right shoes can be the key to believing themselves as the character.

My work of Rudy in *Bent* is a good demonstration of working from the inside out. I worked internally – watching documentaries, visiting the Museum of Tolerance, connecting to the script emotionally, and submerging myself into the inner workings of the character – before working on the **physicality**. Most of the time, working from the inside out worked best for me. However, I once played a sailor from the fifties in a production of Tennessee Williams' play *The Rose Tattoo*, and after struggling for awhile with aspects of the internal work, I finally found him in me when I put on his starched uniform.

There is no "right way" to do this work, so follow your instincts. **Diligence pays off; shortcuts catch up to you**.

The Power of Music

I have heard that Daniel Day-Lewis listened to Eminem between scenes when he worked on *Gangs of New York*. For him, the aggressive nature of that music put him in the space of playing that character. I think it's good to ask yourself what piece of music embodies the energy and world of your character. The song you choose can work as an emotional prep or it may simply put you into the right energetic place. Even finding a piece of music from the time period of the story can be an effective link into that world.

Accents

In this section, you'll find a list of films with specific accents. This is by no means a substitute for going to a dialect coach.

I've created this list primarily because I know that actors are sometimes given an audition with an accent the night before a meeting and have very little time to prepare. In this case, watching a movie with that accent is probably your best bet. I'm also aware that dialect coaches can be expensive and not everyone has the money for this sort of thing. If you can afford it and have the time – especially if you have a callback – spend the money and do it right. Accents can be very complicated and coaching yourself to be authentic and believable in a role can be very challenging, to say the least. It's like singing. Sometimes you don't sound as good as you think and you need some professional guidance or feedback.

People typically learn accents in a relatively systematic way. As you watch these performances, see if you learn best by listening and repeating back, by exploring the character's **physicality**, or by watching the mouth to find the placement and shapes of the sounds. You might find that you even favor a combination of these approaches.

Having the right accent can serve as another way to step into the world of a character. You'll find, if you haven't already, that accents will make you move and feel differently. If you don't believe me, run a monologue using a lower-class Brooklyn accent, then with an upper-class British accent. It's night and day. Accents can free you up almost faster than anything because they're like vocal costumes. If you're looking for more tools to prepare yourself, there are also various online resources to explore. The site **web.ku.edu/idea** has hundreds of recordings of people from all over the world and is one of the best places you can go to research authentic accents. The BBC site **www.bbc.co.uk/voices/recordings** also has a wonderful resource for accents from the UK.

In compiling this list, I've done my best to find films that are current enough to be found at a video store, through a rental service, or on the internet. It includes what I consider to be the most effective examples of accents in films, any of which can be used as research for tone, **physicality**, and overall authenticity. Please understand that while the categories below don't cover every accent from any particular state or country, they do represent the most commonly needed ones in film and television. Here is the list:

- Arabic

    - *Lawrence of Arabia* – Anthony Quinn

- Australian

    - *Candy* – several cast members

    - *Crocodile Dundee 1 & 2* – Paul Hogan

    - *Muriel's Wedding* – Toni Collette & Rachel Griffiths

    - *One Perfect Day* – several cast members

    - *Shine* – several cast members

- Austrian

    - *Inglourious Basterds* – Christoph Waltz

- Boston

    - *The Departed* – Matt Damon and Mark Wahlberg

    - *Good Will Hunting* – Matt Damon and Ben Affleck

    - *Mystic River* – several cast members

- Chinese
    - *Eat Drink Man Women* – several cast members
    - *Face* – several cast members
    - *Joy Luck Club* – several cast members
    - *The Last Emperor* – several cast members
    - *Shanghai Noon* – Jackie Chan
    - *Shanghai Knights* – Jackie Chan
    - *The Wedding Banquet* – several cast members
- Cuban
    - *Scarface* – Al Pacino and several others
- East African
    - *Blood Diamond* - Djimon Hounsou and several others
    - *The Last King of Scotland* – Forest Whitaker
- English – Standard (Received Pronunciation, King's/Queen's English, Oxford English)
    - *Elizabeth* – Cate Blanchett and several others
    - *Madly Deeply* – several cast members
    - *Notting Hill* – Hugh Grant and several others
    - *The Queen* – Helen Mirren and several others
    - *Sense & Sensibility* – several cast members
    - *Shakespeare in Love* – several cast members
    - *V for Vendetta* – several cast members
    - *Venus* – Peter O'Toole and several others

- English – Cockney
    - *Alfie* (1966 version) – Michael Caine
    - *Lock, Stock, and Two Smoking Barrels* – Jason Flemyng and Nick Moran
    - *Sexy Beast* – Ray Winstone and Ben Kingsley
    - *Snatch* – Alan Ford
- English – Liverpool (Liverpudlian, Scouse, Merseyside)
    - *A Hard Day's Night* – several cast members
- English – Manchester
    - *Sparrows Can't Sing* – Rita Tushingham and Dora Bryan
- English – Nottinghamshire
    - *Saturday Night and Sunday Morning* – several cast members
- English – West Country (aka 'pirate')
    - *Pirates of the Caribbean* – Geoffrey Rush and Johnny Depp
    - *Treasure Island* – Robert Newton
- English – Working Class
    - *Snatch* – Jason Statham and several others
    - *Sweeney Todd* – Johnny Depp and Helena Bonham Carter
- English – Yorkshire
    - *Secrets & Lies* – several cast members
- French
    - *Crime Spree* – several cast members
    - *The Da Vinci Code* – Sophie Tautou

- *The Professional* (aka *Leon*) – Jean Reno

- German
  - *The Reader* – David Kross and several others

- Greek
  - *My Big, Fat, Greek Wedding* – several cast members

- Indian
  - *Gandhi* – Ben Kingsley
  - *Slumdog Millionaire* – several cast members

- Irish – Dublin
  - *My Left Foot* – Daniel Day-Lewis and several cast members

- Irish – West Country
  - *Bend It Like Beckham* – Jonathan Rhys Meyers
  - *The Field* – Richard Harris

- Japanese
  - *The Last Samurai* – Ken Watabane and Masato Harada
  - *Only The Brave* – several cast members
  - *White on Rice* – Hiroshi Watanabe

- Mexican
  - Any *Cheech & Chong* movie – several cast members
  - *My Family* (aka *Mi Familia*) – several cast members
  - *El Norte* – several cast members
  - *Selena* – several cast members
  - *The Treasure of the Sierra Madre* – several cast members

- New York
  - *Analyze This* – several cast members
  - *Brighton Beach Memoirs* – several cast members
  - *A Bronx Tale* – several cast members
  - *Do the Right Thing* – several cast members
  - *Fisher King* – Mercedes Ruehl
  - *The Freshman* – several cast members
  - *Frankie & Johnny* – Michelle Pfeiffer (light New York)
  - *Goodfellas* – several cast members
  - *Married to the Mob* – several cast members
  - *Midnight Cowboy* – Dustin Hoffman
  - *Mean Streets* – Harvey Keitel and Robert DeNiro
  - *Moonstruck* – Nicholas Cage and Cher (Brooklyn Italian)
  - *My Cousin Vinny* – Joe Pesci and Marisa Tomei
  - *The Pope of Greenwich Village* – Mickey Rourke and Eric Roberts
  - *Raging Bull* – Robert DeNiro and several others
  - *Saturday Night Fever* – John Travolta
  - *State of Grace* – Sean Penn
  - *Taxi Driver* – Robert DeNiro and several others
  - *World Trade Center* – several cast members
- Persian
  - *The Stoning of Soraya M.* – Shohreh Aghdashloo

- Polish
    - *Sophie's Choice* – Meryl Streep
- Russian
    - *Polly* – Tony Shalhoub
    - *Rounders* – John Malkovich
    - *The Saint* – Rade Serbedzija
- Scottish – Edinburgh
    - *The Last King of Scotland* – James McAvoy
    - *Sliding Doors* – John Hannah
    - *Stone of Destiny* – several cast members
    - *Trainspotting* – Ewan McGregor and several others
- Scottish – Western Isles
    - *Whiskey Galore* (aka *Tight Little Island)* – several cast members
- Scottish – working class
    - *Braveheart* – several cast members
    - *Her Majesty, Mrs. Brown* – Billy Connolly
    - *A Shot at Glory* – Robert Duvall and several others
- South African
    - *Blood Diamond* – Leonardo DiCaprio
    - *District 9* – Sharlto Copley
- Southern – elegant
    - *Forrest Gump* – Sally Fields and several others
    - *Gods & Generals* – Robert Duvall

- *Gone with the Wind* – Vivian Lee

- *Green Mile* – several cast members

- *Jezebel* – Bette Davis

- *My Cousin Vinny* – Fred Gwynne and Lane Smith

- *The Notebook* (subtle) – several cast members

• Southern – working class

- *Junebug* – Amy Adams and several others

- *The Last Picture Show* – several cast members

- *Monster* – Charlize Theron

- *Sling Blade* – Billy Bob Thornton and several others

• Spanish (from Spain)

- *Mask of Zorro* – several cast members

- *Vicky Cristina Barcelona* – Javier Bardem and Penelope Cruz

• Upper Midwest

- *Fargo* – several cast members

• Western

- *Deliverance* – several cast members

- *The Fugitive* – Tommy Lee Jones

- *Rambling Rose* – Laura Dern

- *Tombstone* – several cast members

Yes, there are accent tapes you can buy at theatrical bookstores like Samuel French, but while some may be helpful in teaching you about placement and other technical aspects of the work, you must keep in mind that 99% of the time, the person doing the accent on the tape doesn't actually have the accent. It's always better to listen to the real thing and to work with a coach who can give you immediate feedback.

Lastly, keep in mind that there are several factors that determine which accent a person will have. Economic status must be taken into account as much as geography. Just as a certain type of person from Dallas, Texas may sound completely non-regional, another person from a different economic class in a neighborhood a few miles away may have a strong twang. Again, if you have the time and money, don't hesitate to go to a reputable dialect coach. They can help you clarify the strongest choice based on your character's **given circumstances**.

Background

An associate of mine went to a Q&A session for John Patrick Shanley's *Doubt* and had the opportunity to ask Viola Davis about the extraordinary performance she gave. Somehow, she managed to earn an Oscar nomination for barely eight minutes of screen time with Meryl Streep. He asked her if she had a son in **real life**, and she said no. Did she have a nephew or someone similar that she used? No. So how did she build the deep emotional connection to her son? Her response: "I wrote a fifty-page bio for my character."

What does it mean to create a **background** for your character? The answer is different for everyone. Many actors have the opinion that building **background** is boring, tedious work that has no bearing on their performance. It can be boring, yes, if you're doing it intellectually and just writing useless information. So instead, I would like to encourage you to build an *emotional* **background**. Character **backgrounds**, like the other aspects of this work, are only effective if they stimulate your emotions and connect you to the role in a meaningful way. The process can be very confusing for some, so let me clarify the process.

First, build at least three significant and deeply emotional memories from your character's life. These should be major events that are not necessarily mentioned in the script (those in the script should always be imagined as well – see the chapter on INNER IMAGERY). In other words, create events in your mind's eye that have influenced your character's life. If they're fearful, build fear-based events. If they've had a wonderful marriage, build the perfect wedding until it brings tears to your eyes. Every character walks into a film with a whole life leading up to the here and now, and just like the **moment before**, you need to make it convincing.

Then, go through and answer any unanswered questions the script presents. I've included a chapter of FIFTY CHARACTER QUESTIONS at the back of this book that will help you.

Psychological Gestures

In the film *Capote*, Phillip Seymour Hoffman made several excellent choices for his performance as Truman Capote. One choice in particular was the simple act of how he adjusted and readjusted his glasses – something I suspect he saw the real Capote do in newsreels and whatnot. With all the confidence that character had, there was a bit of awkwardness in the gesture, something uncomfortable. This, along with other strong vocal and physical choices, transported Hoffman and his audiences into the world of Truman Capote. It also won him an Academy Award for best actor.

Coming up with **psychological gestures** that embody your character can be very effective when attempting to morph into someone else. It can add depth to a performance if it's the right choice. You can't just do some random gesture to fulfill this step of the technique; explore choices that illuminate the life and inner workings of your character.

People in real life often exhibit **psychological gestures** when they feel uncomfortable or fearful. I had a student in my class who was working on the play *The Woolgatherer* by William Mastrosimone.

Her character, Rose, is a very fearful person, so I encouraged her to find a gesture to utilize whenever Rose feels panicky. There is a very child-like quality to the character and when we talked about all of the trauma she had experienced, we decided that Rose needed a gesture that would calm her and keep her from feeling out of control. My instinct was for her to go to her hair in some way. The actress I was working with had already made a great choice based on the work she had done: to wear child-like, plastic barrettes in her hair. So I told her to check them whenever she got scared or felt out of control to make sure they hadn't fallen out. The actress also did the additional work of **endowing** her barrettes to make them even more special to her. This **gesture** was the very thing she needed to create originality and sign her work.

Another great example is Cate Blanchett's work as Bob Dylan in the biopic *I'm Not There*. One of the things that riveted me to her performance in this film was her **physicality** – in particular, her **psychological gesture** to rub and touch her lips and face, something she likely got from Dylan himself. This gave an air of insecurity and avoidance that Dylan has in real-life footage. She clearly did her homework and it earned her an Oscar nomination.

Lastly, never get caught. If you watch the performances I've highlighted here, you will see that Hoffman and Blanchett used their gestures with a degree of subtlety, which is to say that the gestures did not take over their performances by becoming an unnecessary focus.

Body Centers & The Alexander Technique

When I was in my teens and early twenties, I was unaware of how walking with my shoulders rolled forward and my chest collapsed was a way of apologizing. Walking around like this was literally like walking around with a big sign that said, "Don't hire me. I'm not ready or good enough." It wasn't until I was screen-testing for the leading role in *Encino Man* that I had a big breakthrough with my own physical insecurities. I was reading for a caveman thrown into modern times and casting requested that we work specifically on the **physicality** of a caveman. I had no idea how do that in an authentic way. I did some research and a friend recommended I work with a man named Jean-Louis Rodrigue. Rodrigue is a master of the *Alexander Technique*, a practice that can be used to create character through **physicality** with as little tension as possible. After a few sessions with him, I had learned a great deal. Although I didn't book the role, I ended up understanding something much more important for my life at that time.

The *Alexander Technique* was so mind-blowing to me that I studied with Rodrigue every week for a period of two years. I began to feel more comfortable in social situations, my income from acting went up substantially and I started booking more and more interesting projects. I never again took the importance of how I carried myself for granted.

Body Centers

Where people lead from says a lot about who they are. The following list will give you an idea of how **body centers** convey important aspects of a person. Many characters break stereotypes, so I encourage you to use these suggestions simply as starting points. Ask yourself, "Based on the **given circumstances**, where does my character lead from?"

- **Leading with the Head** – often smart, driven people who use their intellects to accomplish what they want in the world.

- **Leading with the Nose** – curious, hyper-vigilant, focused, alert types.

- **Leading with the Chin** – proud, cocky, defiant, confrontational, snooty, entitled, upper-class, wealthy business types, old money, *holier than thou* types.

- **Leading with the Shoulders** – guarded, nerdy, self-conscious, afraid, repressed, abused, follower, loner, beaten-down types, etc.

- **Leading with the Chest** – military people, weight lifters, lawyers, execs. Strong, sometimes aggressive people who use power to get what they want in the world. Football players, cocky guys, girls who manipulate with their breasts, warriors, etc.

- **Leading with the Belly** – lazy, backwoods, slobs, food-lovers, working class, family man, fatcat, tycoon, slow, country folk.

- **Leading with the Pelvis** – dancers, models, often confident people who use sex to get what they want, etc.

- **Leading with the Feet** – shy, insecure, small-town, slow, lazy, tired, lower-IQ, etc.

Body Language

Characters, like people, also send clear messages with **body language**. The following are a few of the most common types. Ask yourself, "Based on the **given circumstances**, what does my character say with his or her body?"

- **The Closed-off Body** – when a person is closed off to what's happening around them or being said to them, their bodies typically show it through crossed arms, crossed legs, or looking down or away. Closed-off people often protect themselves by making themselves smaller physically, sometimes caving their chest in and rolling their shoulders forward. Bad posture is common for the closed-off person. A more pragmatic form of closure can be seen when people are cold. Huddling reduces heat loss and to keep the hands warm, people breathe on them, draw them into their chest, sit on them or tuck them under their arms.

- **The Open Body** – when people are open to what's happening around them or what's being said to them, they stand with their arms and legs uncrossed. They may direct their attention solely towards the other person or to their surroundings, their eye contact is likely to be relaxed and prolonged, and they tend to want to be comfortable (removing a jacket or unbuttoning a collar). Good listening is marked by stillness, leaning forward, eye contact with minimal blinking, and the mirroring of the other person's **body language**.

- **The Flirtatious Body** – when people have romantic or sexual interest in others, it can show through prolonged eye contact, preening, caressing their own arms, leg or face, licking and pursing the lips, or interacting with objects in suggestive ways. They may also expose attractive body parts, lean towards the other person, subtly point with a foot, knee, arm or head, move closer to the other person, or imitate the person in some way. They may look at the lips or features of the person they find attractive, or touch the person in some way.

- **The Superior Body** – when people want to give the impression that they're superior, they use their bodies in strong ways. They tend to make their bodies look bigger by placing their hands on their hips, standing upright and erect, lifting the chin and chest, and standing with the feet apart. They flaunt their possessions, casually checking the time on their designer watch, taking out their Mont Blanc pen and telling their assistant to fetch the Havana cigars. They may disrespect others by moving into their personal space, sitting on their chairs, leaning on their cars, putting their feet up on their furniture or being overly-friendly with their romantic partners. They may belittle others by ignoring, interrupting, or turning away from them. Good posture is common for these types of people.

- **The Deceptive Body** – people attempting to deceive others give themselves away inadvertently with sudden movements, minor muscle twitches, changes in vocal tone and speed. In order to avoid being caught, there may be signs of contrived friendly **body language** such as forced smiles. The person may also try to hold their body still, locking their arms to their body in or putting their hands in their pockets. A person who is trying to deceive needs to think more about what they are doing, so they may drift off or pause as they think about what to say or hesitate during speech. Their natural timing may go astray and they may over- or under-react to events. Anxiety may be displaced by actions such as fidgeting, moving around the place or paying attention to unusual things.

Another great way to study **behavior** is to watch people in real life and see if you can figure out what kind of person they are just by how they carry themselves. As you explore physical choices, exaggerate the **body centers** in rehearsal occasionally to see how it makes you feel. Then, when performance time comes, don't let your audience catch you. If you need help with excess body tension, try the EMOTIONAL FOCUS WARM-UP at the end of this book.

Animal Exercises

Choosing a particular animal to represent your character's energy and **physicality** (as I did with the peacock for Rudy in *Bent*) can be transformational. The first step is to look at your character's energy and **worldview** and find an animal that best represents those elements. If you're playing someone who is aggressive, a gorilla or tiger may be appropriate. If you're playing someone who is manipulative who baits people before striking, maybe a cobra fits. Next, study and begin to imitate the animal fully, taking into account its rhythm, focus, stride, **body center**, and even the sounds it makes. Slowly gradate your mimicry down until you end up with an aspect or two that you like. Maybe all you keep is a **psychological gesture** or part of a physical trait. If you choose an owl, you may keep the way its chest sticks out and the sharp way in which they move their heads. Animal work can be really fun and revealing, so give yourself total permission to be physically free with it. Your discoveries can then be integrated into your performance as unique layers.

Secrets

I have heard that Christopher Walken uses a powerful **secret** when he does a scene where he must dominate or intimidate someone. He gives himself the **as if** that he is carrying a gun that he can use whenever he wants to. This simple **secret** gives him the instant power required for those types of scenes, regardless of how he feels on the day of filming.

Secrets can be useful anytime dialogue or **behavior** is unexplained and especially when a scene needs more inner **obstacle** or higher **stakes**. **A secret must not go against the given circumstances, but rather support, justify and deepen your character's behavior.** Let's say you're playing a woman who has a phobia of relationships, and there's no explanation for it in the dialogue or even in the character description. A very effective way of justifying this fear is to come up with a **secret** for your character. Maybe the last man she dated died in a car accident. That's plenty of reason to be scared of falling in love again.

Now let's say you're playing a woman who is abused by her alcoholic spouse. If you're having a hard time justifying why you would stay with him, you could tell yourself that you once tried to commit suicide and he was the one who convinced you to live. This would give you more inner **obstacle** and drastically raise the **stakes** of leaving him. You're not just leaving him; you're leaving the person who saved your life. If you wanted to raise the **stakes** even further, you could give yourself another **secret** that you're pregnant with his child. Leaving him now would also mean leaving your baby without a father, and maybe a bad father would be better than no father at all.

The following are some examples of usable **secrets**:

- A child
- A crush
- A pregnancy

- A personal insecurity

- A sexual event or fantasy

- A marriage or relationship

- A past experience with violence

- A socio-economic issue

- An affair

- An abortion

- An addiction

- An object you're carrying

- The death of a loved one

- Experience with a particular illness (your own or someone else's)

- Something you're wearing under your clothes (lingerie, bullet-proof vest, your grandfather's dog tags, etc.)

So, whenever you find it hard to wrap your head around a particular aspect of a story, give yourself a **secret**. **Secrets** can give you extra fuel, raise the **stakes**, and justify just about anything.

16

FEAR

Creating authentic fear.

Imagine that you've booked the lead in a big budget horror film. The villain is a man with knives for fingers and a face that's burned to a crisp who's out to kill you. In this scene, he chases you through a house after having killed your friends in incredibly painful ways, then bursts through the door to the room where you're hiding. We see the terror on your face as you cry, beg, and say a few lines; then he hacks you up and you die a horrible death.

Here's the thing, though. The actor playing this madman is still in the make-up trailer and the director wants to shoot your close-ups right away, so you've got to act to a piece of tape they've put on the side of the camera while the script supervisor – who is no actress – reads the killer's lines in monotone. Not only that, but the room you're in is filled with crew members, so while you try to prep, the grips are telling jokes, laughing, and having a blast; the hair and make-up people are coming around to do touch-ups on you; and the first A.D. is yelling for people to move to their places.

The camera rolls and the director starts to do his thing. "The door knob is jiggling." You react, but not enough for him. "More emotion! Aaaaand, the door opens!" You react to the piece of tape. "Scream! More desperation!" You say your lines to the tape monster. "Cut! Okay, moving on!" So. How'd you do?

To some, this may sound like a bit of an exaggeration or even a joke. In fact, this is not at all uncommon. They don't make it easy on you, and in order to succeed in these situations, you have to have strong emotional choices in place. This means doing all the work on your own and knowing how to translate the direction you're given.

Getting to Fear

So, what are you afraid of? As an actor, it's a very important question. Death, spiders, clowns, drowning, cancer, being disfigured, losing a parent, being raped, going blind, being tortured? You *will* get auditions that involve fear. It's just a matter of time. So, you must answer this question.

Did you know that more horror films are made every year than any other type of film? Whether you like the genre or not, the auditions are typically some of the most challenging you'll encounter. You often have to go in, read dialogue while reacting to things that aren't there, reach real fear, and break down and beg for your life. How do you do all that and not act? The answer, I believe, is by using technique.

The fear of death – your own or someone else's – is the most common fear for performances. It doesn't matter if it's for a horror film, a psychological thriller, or an action movie, so let's start with that. When people know they're about to die, the first thing that usually occurs to them is to save themselves. As an actor, you have to ask yourself why you want to live. And not wanting to die just on principle is usually not enough. You must be more specific than that.

Do this exercise:

Step One: fill in the blank: "If I died right now, it would devastate me that I wouldn't be able to _____." What goes in the blank? Say goodbye to your mom, hug your dad goodbye, tell someone you're sorry, be successful, have a child, resolve a conflict? If you tend to use your **real life**, this is an important question to pose. If you work more from **imagination**, pose it to your character. Either way, finding the thing you most want to live for is the beginning of getting to fear. Come up with some answers that make you emotional, visualize each one very specifically, and pick the one that moves you most.

Step Two: ask yourself, "What is the worst way I could die?" Being raped and tortured to death? Being stabbed? Being burned alive? Really take your time and explore some choices here. See them, feel them, hear them. If you picture it and it gives you a physical reaction – chills, a sinking feeling in your gut, etc. – as well as an emotional one, it's the right choice. And imagine whatever that horrible death is, it's about to happen to you.

Step Three: create highly emotional images involving what your loved ones go through in the aftermath of your death. See your significant other weep at your grave. See your mother fall to her knees and wail when she finds out how you died. Another option for step three is the **as if** that the killer will go after someone you're very protective of after he's killed you. Visualize your person being murdered in the worst way you can imagine, alone and terrified, struggling to stay alive, tears streaming. Let that affect you.

The most powerful choice from Step One becomes the thing you're fighting for, and the most powerful choice from *either* Step Two or Step Three becomes the thing you're fighting against.

Carbonate yourself fully with the images from Step One, then switch to the thing you're fighting against and see it fully. Create a sentence that expresses your **objective** that you can repeat to yourself. *I have to live, This can't happen,* and *I gotta get out* are all simple, playable inner monologues. If the scene involves you speaking to the person who is about to kill you, you can incorporate him into your inner monologue. *Don't do this, I'll do anything you want,* and *Please don't* are all strong possibilities.

Once you've done the homework on these mental movies and inner monologues, it's time to put them to the test.

1. Remind yourself of why you want to live and see the movie of that happening.

2. Bring up the **inner images** what you're fighting against, seeing all the images and sounds that apply (your mother crying, your father's face, etc.).

3. Let your inner monologue run through your mind a few times or say it quietly to yourself. *Please don't hurt me, I have to live, Please help me, I gotta get out of here,* etc.

4. Launch into the scene with the feeling you just created.

If you've done the work properly and picked strong choices, it should only take a few seconds to bring up the feeling. If it takes more time, go back and pick something stronger.

When presented with a scene where everything is fine at the top and a fear **trigger** comes in the middle, do all the same work but don't play the fear prematurely. If you've done the work properly and made strong choices, the fear should come effortlessly. Do the work and trust that the feeling will be there.

Here's another side note to those actors who are worried that this technique will damage their psyche. Let me assure you that I have done this kind of exercise several times a week for years and have never had anyone be hurt by it. Most of the time, this technique works as a reminder of who is important in our lives. However, as I talked about in EMOTIONAL TRIGGERS, there are some choices that involve **real life** events that you might not be ready to use. Be brave, but also be safe and honest with yourself. If you're having trouble releasing a heavy emotion, see the section on *Letting the Feeling Go* in the chapter EMOTIONAL TRIGGERS.

17

COMEDY

The tips and tricks of funny.

A few years ago, a client set up a coaching session with me to prepare an audition for a sitcom. This actress was experienced with drama and had worked quite a bit in film and television, but when she walked through my door, she was in full-blown panic mode with tears running down her cheeks. "I hate sitcom. I'm not funny, I never have been, and I always bomb these auditions. I wish my agent would stop sending me on this stuff."

I explained to her that just because she didn't understand comedy or hadn't done well with it in the past didn't mean that she would fail. All she needed was technique in that area. I asked her what her **objective** in the scene was, she looked at me with skepticism, and off we went. By the end, after applying the technique and coming up with some fun comedic choices, we were having a blast. She left for the audition, not with complete confidence, but with enough to know she wouldn't blow it. I got a phone call later that day announcing her callback, and although she didn't get that role, she booked the lead on a sitcom shortly thereafter.

During her first year on the show, she came in every week to break down each new episode. Once she fully understood the character and the technique, she began to break them down by herself. After the show became a huge hit, I asked her, "So, are you funny?"

With a wry smile she replied, "Yeah, I guess I am."

Comedy Technique

I often hear people say that comedy can't be learned; people are either funny or they're not. This is only half-true. Yes, one in a hundred actors has a natural gift for comedy, but the rest of us can tap in as well. Like anything else, it can be learned. I can't tell you how many times students have told me they're not good at comedy and it turned out they just didn't understand it.

Speaking of which, let's start with the misconception that comedy is about showing off or trying to be funny. If you feel the impulse to try to be funny, resist it. Audiences will spot it immediately. Sometimes you'll know something is funny when you read it, but when it comes to performances, you must play the reality of the situation your character is in. The common denominator is finding the underlying truth of what your character is struggling through. All great comedies have an element of truth that you as the actor must find and share with the audience.

In the next few pages, we'll explore what I believe are the most important elements of comedy technique. However, while my aim is to teach you how to be the greatest comedic actor you can be, we must acknowledge the fact that, just like with accents, no book could ever fully accomplish this. I encourage you, after learning everything you can from this chapter, to seek out a coach who truly knows comedy and who will allow you to put what you've learned into use in a classroom or one-on-one setting.

Getting into a Playful Mindset

Comedy is a playful game. After all the breaking down and technique work is over, it's about letting go, being in the moment, working off your partner(s), and having fun.

Hopefully you'll have the privilege of working with a director that lets you explore different **behavior** and line choices. My experience has been that most of the greatest moments in comedy happen without being planned as such. The actors, having done all their work, were given the permission to play.

Improvising dialogue is commonly used during shooting on big films and shows like *The Office* to help make performances fresh. Leads typically have more freedom with this than supporting actors do, so always tread lightly and ask before improvising. Know also that sitcom actors, more than film actors, have to stick to the script because the jokes in them are usually written more technically than in comedic movies. Whatever the case, it's your job to bring the fun and enjoy that playful mindset.

When I was a young actor, I spent too much time taking myself seriously in comedy, which was a problem. The actors who typically book the jobs are chosen because their love of play is intoxicating. Somehow, they're there not only there to audition but to do what they love to do. Those are the people that executives want to be around and hire. It took me years to understand that and I want you to learn it now.

I once had the opportunity to watch Mike Myers work on set and what impressed me most was his passion for trying new things and the joy he brought to the work. He would do several takes of a single scene and run to the monitors between each one to see how his choices worked. Eventually, sometimes as many as twenty takes later, he would joyfully announce, "I think we got it!" Obviously, it's a bit more difficult to do this sort of thing if you're not a celebrity with full freedom, but I learned something very important by watching him. **A comedic genius is someone with technique, lots of ideas, and the freedom to play.**

I had the same experience when I visited a client on the set of a Jim Carrey movie. Carrey's playfulness was amazing. He told jokes, sang between takes, and when it came time to roll the camera, he became focused and ready to explore within the framework of his choices. That's an idea I talk about a lot in this book because I believe it's always the end goal: to let go and trust the homework.

Comedy Core Traits

Put a sensitive, nervous, anal-retentive hermit in a room with a carefree, sloppy, poker-playing optimist and comedy is likely to follow.

Adjectives like these – anal-retentive, carefree, sloppy, etc. – make up what I call **core traits** in comedy, which you must work to uncover for any comedic character you play. To be clear: "character" means *real person*, not caricature. All great comedies have very specific, heightened characters and each of them has something distinctive that sets them apart from the others. These heightened **core traits** remind us of how absurd people can really be.

When dealing with comedy, work first to understand how your character is distinctive. Why are they in the story and what would be missing if they were omitted? Come up with a few descriptive words for your character like smart, dumb, lovable loser, paranoid, rational, weird, neurotic, perverted, lazy, innocent, talkative, materialistic, nervous, slutty, womanizing, neat, uptight, prude, messy, bitchy, brutally honest, prissy, etc. This process is similar to the work involved in **emotional relationship**, except that you're coming up with descriptions for your own character. When working on a role, it's best to find these traits from the clues in the character breakdown, stage directions, and dialogue. Here is a list of great characters from sitcoms and their **core traits**:

Seinfeld

- Kramer played by Michael Richards – energetic eccentric
- Jerry played by Jerry Seinfeld – sardonic, rational one
- George played by Jason Alexander – high-strung, neurotic loser
- Elaine played by Julia Louis-Dreyfus – abrasive, neurotic serial-dater

Will & Grace

- Grace played by Debra Messing – self-absorbed neurotic
- Karen played by Megan Mullally – entitled, pill-popping drunk
- Jack played by Sean Hayes – mischievous clown
- Will played by Eric McCormack – pragmatic fixer
- Rosario played by Shelley Morrison – harsh voice of reason

Everybody Loves Raymond

- Debra played by Patricia Heaton – stressed-out, responsible one
- Raymond played by Ray Romano – childish, loveable loser

30 Rock

- Tracy played by Tracy Morgan – dumb celebrity
- Liz Lemon played by Tina Fey – pragmatic, nerdy voice of reason
- Kenneth played by Alex McBrayer – naïve, moral one
- Jack Donaghy played by Alec Baldwin – corporate know-it-all
- Jenna played by Jane Krakowski – self-absorbed, ditzy diva

Friends

- Joey played by Matt LeBlanc – dumb slut

- Ross played by David Schwimmer – loveable loser
- Phoebe played by Lisa Kudrow – blissful eccentric
- Chandler played by Matthew Perry – wise-cracking little boy
- Monica played by Courtney Cox – maternal neurotic

The Office – U.S. Cast

- Michael Scott played by Steve Carell – clueless visionary
- Jim Halpert played by John Krasinski – straight man

Scrubs

- JD played by Zach Braff – quirky romantic
- Dr. Perry Cox played by John C. McGinley – harsh narcissist

Old-School Sitcoms

- Archie Bunker in *All in the Family* played by Carroll O'Connor – loveable, prejudiced know-it-all
- Carla in *Cheers* played by Rhea Perlman – no-nonsense, short-tempered, bossy one
- Woody in *Cheers* played by Woody Harrelson – big-hearted simpleton
- Sam in *Cheers* played by Ted Danson - vain womanizer
- The Fonz in *Happy Days* played by Henry Winkler – suave rebel
- Lucy in *I Love Lucy* played by Lucille Ball – mischievous dreamer
- Ricky Ricardo in *I Love Lucy* played by Desi Arnaz – straight, rational one
- Al Bundy in *Married with Children* played by Ed O'Neill – pathetic, doomed everyman
- Kelly in *Married with Children* played by Christina Applegate – dumb slut

- Mork from *Mork & Mindy* played by Robin Williams – energetic eccentric

- Jack in *Three's Company* played by John Ritter – loveable, clutzy playboy

Of course, many of these **comedy core traits** are open to debate, but this hopefully gives you a clear idea of what **core traits** are and how to identify them within comedy scripts. Understand also that the longer the show runs, the more the writers will play with and expand the **core traits** of the characters. *Friends* is a prime example of a show where the characters had to evolve over time and even switch some **core traits**. Regardless, all great comedy characters start out with clear traits that make them distinctive, loveable in some way, and funny.

Core Traits in Action

In his wonderful play *The Odd Couple*[4], Neil Simon pairs up the neurotic Felix and the laid-back Oscar as roommates. At the top of Act III, the stage direction tells us, *"Felix enters from the hallway with a vacuum cleaner and begins doing a thorough job on the rug."* This indicates how he's extremely particular about cleanliness. He isn't just cleaning the rug; he's doing a thorough job. *"Oscar takes a cigar out of his pocket and as he crosses in front of Felix to the couch, he unwraps it and drops the wrapping carelessly on the floor."* This is one of many examples of descriptive stage direction that clearly points to him being messy, and it's easy to imagine the conflict that will follow.

Further into Act III, Felix tells us everything we need to know about Oscar. "You're a wonderful guy, Oscar… You're also one of the biggest slobs in the world… and completely unreliable… undependable… and irresponsible." In just a few short sentences, any

---

[4] Published by Samuel French, Inc., 1966

actor auditioning for Oscar will know that he needs to take those descriptions into account when building his character.

These two personalities are prime examples of how valuable and common opposing **core traits** are in comedy writing. Always look for opposites; they are a staple in this genre. If you are at all confused about your character's **core traits**, look at the **traits** of the other person in the scene and yours will likely be the opposite. Here are some examples of pairings:

• Smart & Dumb

• Prissy & Promiscuous

• Clean & Messy

• Easy-Going & Uptight

• Materialistic & Cheap

• Timid & Risky

• Neurotic & Rational

• Lazy & High-Energy

Whether you're working on comedy in film, TV, or theatre, always identify your **core traits**. All other choices stem from there.

Note: If you originate a role in a play, the stage direction in the script will come directly from the writer as hints to the character's inner workings. Otherwise, the stage direction you read might be the original actor's interpretation and not the writer's intent. In this case, take the stage direction with a grain of salt; the actor may have been brilliant or gone astray. For the purposes of this section, I took the stage directions from The Odd Couple *as original.*

The Straight One

Sometimes you'll play the straight one or the smart, rational one, not the blatantly funny one. If this is the case, still mine for the jokes, but don't try to over-think or out-shine the funny characters. Your job is to set up the punch lines most of the time. Straight characters are usually the voice of reason and often reflect what the audience is thinking. They have the most common sense of the bunch and often use sarcasm to state their opinions and drive their points home. Many great sitcoms feature the wife as the straight, rational one and the husband as the lovable loser. Some prime examples of a good 'straight man/woman' are Patricia Heaton on *Everybody Loves Raymond,* Helen Hunt on *Mad About You*, Donna Pinciotti on *That '70s Show*, Desi Arnaz on *I Love Lucy*, and Eric McCormack on *Will & Grace*. The straight one will typically be a female, but not always. If this is your character, you can still be funny, but it will usually come from your reactions to the crazies around you.

Research

As with any show, film, or play, it's important to understand the size and style of the material on which you're working. You must always do your research. Some shows are fast-paced and others take their time. Some are edgy and others are silly. Some single camera shows like *30 Rock* and *The Office* have a very real, film-like feel, while *Will & Grace* or *Seinfeld* can sometimes feel larger than life. If it's a TV show currently on the air, watch an episode. Otherwise, see if you can find the show online. Whatever you're working on, garnish as much as you can from the writing and find details about the people involved with the project.

In the end, no matter how much information you acquire, you must commit and make creative choices. Don't be afraid to be silly or outrageous and remember to bring something unique to every role you play.

Behavior & Physical Choices

In the play *Cheaters*[5], by Michael Jacobs, lovers Michelle and Allen come home from a wedding where Allen caught the bridal bouquet and then threw it back, a gesture that humiliated Michelle. She feels he should've given it to her and all her insecurities about not being desired spill out. After all, she was the only unmarried girl there.

While Michelle is the nervous, needy neurotic who wants to be married, Allen is the childish, content bachelor, who wants things to stay the way they are. The conflict is easy to see. Here we have another writer who has pitted opposing **objectives**, **comedy core traits**, and rigid points of view against each other. **Behavior** and physical choices are born out of these factors.

At the beginning of the scene, Michelle locks Allen out of their apartment and he tries to convince her to let him back in. A smart actor will find creative ways of trying to get her to open the door, rather than just reading the dialogue from the hallway. One particular actor who did this scene in my class made some great choices for his opening lines in this scene. "Open up or you will be denied my reassuring masculinity... to protect you from the creature that hides under the bed" inspired him to make a scary monster sound that is not written in the script. For the lines, "Okay, I'm going, here's the elevator, I'm going... I'm in the lobby," he allowed his voice to become further away and more muffled as he went. A handkerchief appeared under the door and waved around like a flag of surrender before the line "Look. It's late. I'm tired. I want to get out of these clothes." When the actress finally opened the door after hearing, "STELLA! Hey, STELLA," it was to find him on his knees. He was mimicking the pose Marlon Brando took in *A Streetcar Named Desire*, the film from which that line was taken. An amateur actor may not even understand that reference or research it. The smart

---

[5] Published by Samuel French, Inc., 1982

actor, even if he didn't recognize the famous line, would look it up online – once again, an amazing tool for researching.

Choices like the ones made by this actor may seem obvious to you, but I can't tell you how many times I've watched actors with less experience do a scene with generic choices or even with no choices at all. It's up to you to mine the **given circumstances** to find your **comedy core traits**, needs, point of view, occupation and place, and create **behavior** based on that information. If explored creatively, no two actors should ever do a scene the same way.

Sitcom

Sitcom is concentrated comedy: twenty-two minutes of show time broken up by eight minutes of commercials. Typically, there are at least three jokes per page and they are all very specific. There's still a lot of room for interpretation in the physical comedy and line delivery, but for the most part, it's the most technical format for comedies, and is even more technical than drama. For many people, it's the hardest thing to learn if they're not good at it naturally which, as I've said, is probably one out of every hundred actors.

I developed these guidelines through trial and error, conversations with comedy writers, and by doing coachings with comedically talented clients. The truth is that as technically difficult as this stuff is, when you know what you're doing, it can be the most enjoyable material to perform. While collaboration and feedback from professionals are invaluable, I believe the ideas we're about to explore will help you enormously.

How to Identify a Sitcom Script

Many actors have a hard time telling if an audition they're going out on is a sitcom or not. Traditional sitcom has a very specific format and can easily be identified by its double-spaced dialogue running down the center of the page, like so:

STACY OPENS THE PANTRY DOOR AND FINDS TERRY SITTING
ON THE FLOOR, SCARFING DOWN COOKIES.

                    STACY

        Terry! I though you said you were

        going on a diet.

                    TERRY

        Yeah, I was thinking of maybe

        starting that tomorrow when I'm

        done craving cookies.

This format is not to be confused with double-spaced soap opera material, which runs down the left-hand side of the page.

Heightened Life

Sitcom is based in reality but played on a larger scale. When you're working correctly, it can often feel a bit over-the-top. Reactions and situations all tend to be exaggerated. This means that when characters are excited about something, they're really, really excited. If they're upset, they're extremely upset. Emotions should always be authentic but amped-up for a character in this genre.

Stick to the Script

For the most part, as I said before, you must keep the lines as they are written in a sitcom. Dialogue and punctuation are very important here. Subtle changes like adding a small word or phrase where it doesn't belong or ignoring punctuation can kill jokes and disrupt the rhythm of the writing. So, when you have auditions for sitcom, you must always stick to the script and, whenever possible, memorize the lines. Here are some guidelines for you to follow:

- Periods are most often quick stops. The writer is telling you to pause. Just be mindful that you don't allow the energy and rhythm of the piece to fall flat.

- Commas are very slight pauses. Other times, the writer has included them simply because they're grammatically correct.

- Questions really do mean they want you to ask this question. These sentences should never be said like a statement.

- Exclamation points are used to show joy, anxiety, excitement, and frustration! You don't have to raise your voice, but there's an importance and intensity to the line that needs to be there. The line should have a strong **thought** or **intention** attached to it.

- Words that are underlined, italicized, bolded, or written in all capital letters require extra emphasis. It's either the setup for a joke or the joke itself. Just as with exclamation points, raising your voice isn't always necessary, but emphasis is.

- Ellipses (…) in the middle of lines are pauses and are typically used for momentary stumbles in the character's thought process. In these cases, you don't know what you're going to say until you say it.

- Dashes at the end of a line indicate that your character is being cut off either by someone else or by another **thought**. If it's the former, be sure to know what the rest of the sentence is – one to four words is usually best – in case the other actor or casting director doesn't cut you off. If you're supposed to cut the other character off, be sure you do so.

No Handles

Handles are small words that actors sometimes add without knowing that they're impeding the rhythm of the piece. They think they're making the dialogue more real or conversational. While

handles can be very useful in drama or even in comedic movies, they are usually deadly when employed in sitcom. Again, always stick to the script. Some common examples:

- Like
- Uh
- So
- Well
- Listen

- Look
- Hey
- Yo
- Man (as in, "Man, what's your deal?")

Vitality and Pace

Most comedy is fast-paced and sitcom is no exception. This doesn't mean you should say everything as fast as you can. It means you must do your best to pick up your cues, get to the end with energy and vitality, and avoid taking pauses in the middle of a line when the script doesn't specify one. Forgetting these things can kill the comedy in a scene. Be sure to rehearse comedy out loud and on your feet whenever possible. Sitting on a cozy chair works against the energy and rhythm required for a sitcom.

Sadness and Anger

When working on sitcom, it's rarely a good idea to convey sadness or anger in a realistic way. These emotions, when displayed authentically, will turn your sitcom into a drama. Instead of thinking of your character as sad, think of her as overwhelmed. Instead of angry, think frustrated. It can even help when working on the material in rehearsal to say out loud, "This is so frustrating!" Then let out a sound of frustration and go into the lines you perceive as angry. Try, "I'm so overwhelmed" for the sad lines.

Most people, once they begin to understand this, can tap into the replacement emotions easily. For obvious examples of this, watch great, traditional sitcoms like *Will & Grace*, *Friends*, or *Seinfeld*.

Thoughts

This is one of the most effective tools for strong comedic acting and no matter what level you're on, making use of it will improve your work. A **thought** before a line complements sitcom dialogue and provides a way to be specific in the same way **intentions** work for drama. **Intentions** can also be used in comedy, but with sitcom, **thoughts** are even more crucial. They help you to make specific choices that affect your character's tone, color, and subtext. Much of this method will need to be learned through trying different choices to see what works for your characters and what doesn't.

Let's take the simple line, "Where'd you get that shirt?" The number of **thoughts** that could work before this line are endless outside the context of a script, but try the following and see how the line changes with each:

- *Sweeeeeet.*

- *What's up, sexy?*

- *What the...*

- *Ew.*

- *Oh. My. God.*

- *Wait a second.*

- *You thief!*

Here are some simple guidelines for creating **thoughts**:

- Don't forget your **objective**. Engaging your character's **objective** while creating and then employing your **thoughts** creates the balance of specificity and drive that comedy needs in order to make people laugh.

- **Thoughts** are often light-hearted in nature.

    - *Oh shit, Mommy!, Ew, Hellooooo, Holy crap, What the hell was her name,* etc.

- They are almost never angry.

    - *Screw you, I hate you,* etc.

- Sounds can also be used as **thoughts**, if they're authentic and funny.

    - *Ooooooo!, AAAAhhh!!, ugh,* etc.

- They should be quick and have some kind of feeling in them, not too long or intellectual.

    - The **thought** *I have to figure out how to get out of here* could be changed to *Kill me now.*

- They work best when they're different from the line they precede, rather than a short-form version of the line itself.

- You will be most effective when you experiment with three or more **thoughts** that could work and then pick the best one.

- Don't try to be funny. Play the reality of what the character is going through.

Reversal

A **reversal** – also known as a **turnaround** – is when a character changes <u>abruptly</u> from one emotion to another. From excited to confused, from frustrated to fake casual, from friendly to hostile, from happy to really scared, etc. Here are some simple examples:

- "Yeah, cool, bungee jumping sounds amazing! Are you out of your mind?!"

- "Are you kidding? I've dated SO many women… I have no idea what I'm doing."

- "I am so not afraid of you. Please don't hurt me!"

Recoveries

A **recovery** is when a character tries to make up for something that shouldn't have been said or done and can be thought of as a kind of gradual **reversal**.

KATHY IS ABOUT TO OPEN THE CLOSET WHERE JOHN IS HIDING HIS DRUNK FRIEND.

                    JOHN

          (TERRIFIED) NO, DON'T! I mean...

          (SLOWLY FORCING A SMILE) it's... just

          so dirty in there; I wouldn't want

          you to see that.

Covering

Sitcom characters often **cover** their **thoughts** or emotions, but not enough that the audience can't see them underneath. This is another reason why **thoughts** can be so useful in comedy. Regardless of what the character is saying, we can see the truth of the **thought** behind every line.

JODY SNEAKS IN AFTER A NIGHT OF PARTYING, SHE TRIES TO MAKE IT THROUGH THE HOUSE UNNOTICED. HER FATHER FLICKS ON THE LIGHT.

                    KATHY

          Hey, dad. How was your night?

By using the **thought** *OH SHIT!* just before the line, you create an internal terror that the audience will see. If you then **cover** it up for your dad by smiling and saying your line, you embody more of a sitcom feel.

Over-articulation

Over-articulating the right line of dialogue can be very funny.

* "What don't you understand?!" Give every consonant far more attention and importance than you normally would as if you're speaking to a complete moron.

Comedy Scoring

The following scene is a great example of a sitcom script. It was written by a professional comedy writer and friend of mine, David Holden. As you can see from the hints in the dialogue, Jenine is the straight one while Trevor is the insecure gym-oholic. Although this example doesn't address all aspects of comedy, the **thoughts** and other parts of the technique I've written in will give you a good idea of how these tools work. When it comes to **thoughts**, I encourage you to explore two or three before picking your favorite for each line.

INT. BEDROOM - NIGHT

TREVOR ENTERS IN SWEATY WORKOUT CLOTHES CARRYING HIS GYM BAG. JENINE READS SOME WORK-RELATED STUFF IN BED.

Help me.   TREVOR

          Ooh! Ooh! Ooh!

JENINE   *Heeeere we go.*

Let me guess. Leg workout this

evening?

Total nightmare.   TREVOR

You know in horror movies how

coffins make that squeaking sound

when they open? That's the sound my

knees made on my last set of

squats.

JENINE   *Hellooooo?*

Which could be a sign that you're

spending a tad too much time at the

gym.

No biggie.   TREVOR   ⇓ *Hey, baby.*

Well, no pain, no gain. So you in

the mood for a little (WHILE TRYING

REVERSAL to   ←*COVER w/*

Oh God →   TO SIT DOWN) Ow, ow, ow (THEN) Sexy *I'm cool.*

time?

JENINE   *(sarcastic) Yeah, right.*

Sure. I think I have a nurse outfit

around here somewhere… because you

need medical attention. Seriously,

you're overdoing it.

SHE EXITS.

You're lucky!   TREVOR

                    (YELLS OFF) Only because I care.

                              JENINE   *Let's be real.*

          About what? The way you look.

JENINE ENTERS WITH A BAG OF FROZEN PEAS.

                              JENINE (CONT'D)   *This is*
                                                  ridiculous!
          The only way to spend more time

          with you is to be a barbell!

          Come on.   TREVOR

          Sweetheart, you're over-reacting.

Son of a... → (GRABBING LEGS) Seriously I think

          my legs are falling off.

SHE SLAPS THE FROZEN PEAS ON HIS LEG.

                              TREVOR (CONT'D)
          AAAAA!!   *Sweet relief.* ⇓
                    Coldy, cold! (THEN) Ahhhh. (THEN)
I'm ready. So we gonna do it or what?

                              JENINE   *Funny.*

          That's a good question. Cause I

          don't know <u>what</u> we're doing. I

          thought you moved in here so we

          could take our relationship to the

          next level. I didn't realize the

next level was you being at the gym

all day. Trev, I really think you

have relationship issues.

Thanks a lot.   TREVOR

Well, now the mood's ruined.

                        JENINE   *(mocking) Oh bummer.*

Really? You think? Because here's a

little secret. (WHISPERS) You never

had a chance.

Well, excuuuuuse me.   TREVOR

Forgive me for wanting to keep in

shape so we can keep our romance

alive.

                        JENINE
                                Seriously?

Don't try and make it like you're

doing this for us. Since when is

obsessing over what your body looks

like romance?

You're gonna be sorry.   TREVOR

Okay... I swore I'd never do this

but... I want to show you

something. And when I say I, I mean

you, cause I can't move. It's under

the bed.

               JENINE   *Okaaayyyyy...*

(LOOKING UNDER THE BED) What am I

looking for?

               TREVOR

Shoot me now.

A blue photo album. They say a

picture is worth a thousand words,

well this is worth a million. Very

few people have seen this picture.

In fact, I'm really thinking about

having you sign a confidentiality

agreement.

JENINE PULLS A PHOTO ALBUM OUT FROM UNDER THE BED.

               JENINE   *What the hell?*

Trev, you're freaking me out. Are

your clothes on in this picture? Is

everyone's clothes on?

TREVOR TAKES THE PHOTO ALBUM AND FLIPS TO A CERTAIN
PAGE. JENINE LOOKS AT THE PICTURE. HER JAW DROPS.

               TREVOR

I know!

Yes, yes, unfortunately yes. That's

me on prom night.

JENINE   *You're huge!*

(OFF PHOTO) Oh my God.

It gets worse.   TREVOR

My sister took that picture. She

was also my date. As you can see by

the buttons on my shirt that were

struggling to stay on... I was two

hundred and fifty pounds. On the

bright side, I did say no to drugs.

Sadly I couldn't do the same with

Cheetos. My fingers are still a

little orange.

JENINE   *Aw, baby.*

I can't believe this. How come you

never told me about this?

I don't know.   TREVOR

Cause it's horrible, I'm

embarrassed about it, I wanted you

to like me, I mean pick one. The

possibilities are endless.

JENINE   *Wow.*

I'm in shock.

                          TREVOR

This stinks.

          Do you hate me now? Should I move

          out? Are we never having sex again?

SHE STARTS UNBUTTONING HER SHIRT WITH A SMILE.

     Holy...   TREVOR (CONT'D)

          Wow. Really? I woulda pulled that

          thing out earlier. I never thought

          that picture had such aphrodisiac

          qualities.

THEY KISS. THEY TURN OUT THE LIGHT. AFTER A BEAT, IN
THE DARKNESS WE HEAR:

     Ow Ow!!   TREVOR (CONT'D)

          Charlie Horse!

A Final Note About Comedy

Regardless of how much natural ability you do or do not have
with comedy, practicing these tools will boost your skills and
confidence. If comedy happens to be your career focus, find a class or
an improv company that inspires you and get on stage as much as
possible. Remember that being a comedic genius is about more than
just natural ability. Rather, it's about having technique, lots of ideas, a
strong work ethic, and the freedom to play.

18

DRUGS & ALCOHOL

Creating drug- and alcohol-induced performances.

In order to write this chapter, I did extensive research on all of these drugs, including calling up memories of when I experimented with many of them back in high school. Understand that everyone reacts to drugs in different ways based on their history, method of use, dosage, frequency of use, environment, and psychology. I haven't done any of these drugs in over twenty years, and I'm convinced that you don't have to in order to get to the feeling or to understand why people use them.

Understanding a drug does not take the place of doing all the other work for the character. Always remember that you can't bypass the other parts of technique just because you have mastered the effects or induced **behavior** of a drug. Also keep in mind that you don't want to play-act these drugs. The provided exercises should give you an understanding of the feelings and **behaviors** these drugs produce so you can create a truthful, memorable performance.

In order to give you a deeper and more compassionate understanding of the user, it's very important to observe people who are on the drug, whether in real life or in the films or documentaries listed in this chapter. Combining observation with research will help to clue you in to the way your character takes the drug and what affects it has. Then, once you've settled on a method for getting to the feeling that works for you, trust it and don't overplay it. No matter how drunk or high the character is, authentic subtlety is always better than an exaggerated façade. Like so many other components of the technique, your drug work should always complement your performance, not overpower it. Enjoy the work, and if you feel the effects of these exercises lasting longer than you intended, or if you find the emotions hard to shake, see the section on *Letting the Feeling Go* in the chapter EMOTIONAL TRIGGERS.

Alcohol

Water, tea, and apple juice are the three most common substitutions for alcohol in performances. Adding a small amount of lemon juice or vinegar can be helpful to give the drink some bite.

Psychology of a True Alcoholic

- Once the first drink is picked up, you can't stop until you pass out, run out of money, or get cut off. One is too many; a hundred isn't enough.

- The next drink is all you think about even when you're not drinking. A night without alcohol sounds completely uninteresting and always turns out as such. The inner monologue is often:

    - *Oh man, I could really use a drink.*

- You're convinced that you drink due to the circumstances of your life.

- You use any reason to get drunk, good or bad.

  - *I need a pick-me-up.*
  - *I need it to wind down.*
  - *It helps me be more myself.*
  - *It's the beginning of the week.*
  - *It's the end of the week.*
  - *It helps me be creative.*
  - *I'm better at things when I have a buzz.*

- Anyone who drinks less than you is weak, while anyone who drinks more has a problem.

- You need your glass to be full at all times. Anxiety can set in quickly when you can't get a bartender's attention.

- No matter where you are, you always want to be some place else.

- You think everyone else sees you as the most fascinating person in the room, but you feel like a piece of shit at the center of the universe.

- You can't imagine life without alcohol. What else is there?

- Alcohol is a friend who helps you through life.

Behavior and Rituals

I. If your character is a social drinker rather than a full-blown alcoholic, skip directly to section II of *Behavior and Rituals*. If your character is a true alcoholic, consider incorporating the following:

- You always have alcohol hiding somewhere nearby.

- You never leave a drink half-empty.

- You mix alcohol in with other beverages: coffee, soda, tea, juice, etc.

- You can become compulsive about anything.

- Swirling the ice in the glass, sipping slowly.

- You might have a couple drinks at home before going out and very specific music you listen to while getting ready. You may pour a drink into a flask to take with you.

- In an effort to appear sober, adopt a wide stance or use a nearby fixed object, such as a table or a wall, to keep yourself stable.

- You hide the smell that even lingers when you're sober by:

  - Wearing perfume or cologne.
  - Using mints, gum, or candy.
  - Keeping your distance from others.

- For some, there is very little stillness. The hands are always busy:

  - Flipping a lighter.
  - Peeling labels off bottles.
  - Doodling on napkins while pretending to have big thoughts because you feel like everyone's watching you.

II. Whether your character is a true alcoholic or a social drinker, consider the following:

- Determine what kind of drunk your character is: happy, angry, flirty, depressed, sentimental, pensive, aloof.

- What kind of drink does your character prefer? How do they order or make it? Part of your character's psychology matches the drink they drink. There's an image that comes with specific types of drinks. Working-class people tend to drink things like beer and whiskey while upper crust people tend to go for martinis and fine wine.

- You may be very specific about the alcohol you want. This specificity diminishes the more inebriated you become.

- Simple tasks – like counting out the proper amount of change, buttoning a shirt, or finding the right key for your front door and putting it in the lock – require your utmost concentration and take much longer than usual.

- You have no sense of personal boundaries – your own or those of others – and can easily become overly-familiar and inappropriate with strangers, sometimes making a fool of yourself without knowing it.

- If you're overly intoxicated, you may intend to walk directly towards someone or something you're looking at, but end up veering off in another direction entirely.

- You may become sloppy, disheveled or careless under the influence. Maybe your hair is messy, your clothes are in disarray, or you attempt dangerous stunts you would normally avoid.

- When interacting with others, either find other things to look at the entire time or be inexorably focused on the other person.

Creating the Feeling

Remember always do the necessary homework on your character first and never to over-play the drunk. Remember, your drug work should always complement your performance, not overpower it.

- While standing, relax your body, letting go of any tension you may be holding, especially in your stomach. Most of us walk around holding our stomachs in. Release it.

- Blur your vision into soft focus. You may be able to do this without thinking about it. If not, either take your focus from what you're looking at around to the back of the eyes or find the balance between regular focus and having your eyes crossed.

- Drunks rarely have a reliable center of balance; they're either back on their heels or forward on their toes. So, while in soft focus, relax your knees slightly and slowly move your center of gravity forward on your toes, keeping your heels on the ground for the most part. Then move backwards onto your heels without lifting your toes too much. Sway back and forth and even slightly side to side. You may even fall and have to catch yourself. Let this happen. Explore this step of the exercise for a minute or two.

- Next, walk around with your center of balance switching from you heels to toes and back again. If you're sure it's safe, let yourself bump into things. Stumble around the room for a minute or so.

- When you fully feel the effects, incorporate the emotional state of your drunk (sad, angry, etc. See section II of *Behavior and Rituals* for more information) and walk around. Drop something and try to pick it up. Notice how hard that is.

- If you need another boost into the feeling, an optional step is to spin around in a circle three to six times with your eyes still in soft focus.

- Improvise an inner monologue like the ones provided later in this section or go to the script.

- The last step is to work to overcome the handicaps you've given yourself. Most drunks do their best to appear sober, meaning they actively try to focus through their blurry vision and stand up straight in spite of their unreliable center of balance.

Choosing to be a subtle drunk is often best. So, once you feel fully drunk, gradate it down till you get to your character's tipsy state. The more you have done the exercise, the easier it will be to trigger yourself to the feeling. After working on it enough, you may just need to start shifting your balance or move into soft focus in order to feel the effects.

Slur

Not all drunks have problems speaking, but if you're playing a character that is extremely drunk, you may want to incorporate a slur. If the first part of this exercise doesn't naturally impede your speech, try the following.

- Imagine that your tongue has been tranquilized. It is now just a useless lump in your mouth, making it difficult to talk or swallow properly.

- As you speak, work to consciously swallow and actively overcome the speech impediment. Try to sound as though there's nothing wrong with your speech by using your lips to articulate around your useless, tranquilized tongue.

- Improvise an inner monologue like the examples below or go to the script.

Inner Monologue When It's Good

- Every night feels like *the* night.
  - *Tonight's gonna be the night.*
- You're ready for anything.
  - *Here we go, baby.*
- You feel like you're looking good, you always have the right thing to say, you're incredibly witty, and you flirt better than anyone around.
  - *I got this.*
  - *You know you like me.*
- You feel the permission to be sentimental. Everyone is amazing.
  - *I love you guys so much.*

Inner Monologue When It's Bad

- A strong feeling of self-loathing takes you over.
  - *I'm fucking fucked.*
  - *This is over. I'm done with this.*
  - *Oh God, please fucking help me. I hate this shit.*

- *Please God help me, somebody fucking help me. I don't want to do this anymore.*
- *Oh God, not this again.*
- *I'm going to die.*

- The room spins horribly around you, nausea sets in and you throw up.
- Everyone else is to blame for everything that goes wrong.
- You feel very aggressive and depressed at the same time.

Withdrawal Effects of a Casual User

The social drinker will tend to experience a typical hangover the next day, consisting of a headache, nausea, fatigue, slow movement, sensitivity to light and sound, and sometimes even feelings of depression.

Withdrawal Effects of a True Alcoholic

- You'll have to pick up your life where you left off before you started drinking. Every emotion you've suppressed for as long as you've been drinking will slam into you all at once. You'll feel like you don't know what you're doing at your job, in your relationships, etc.
- You'll either have no appetite or an insatiable need for food.
- You'll experience intense sugar cravings because of alcohol's high sugar content, so you may keep candy on you for a sugar fix.
- You'll have an oral fixation. If you're a smoker, you'll smoke more than usual.
- You'll be absentminded and forgetful.
- Going to Alcoholics Anonymous brings a horribly lonely feeling.
  - *No one can possibly know how I feel.*

- Your addiction is a monster doing pushups in the corner while you try to build your strength and live a life that's suddenly very difficult.

- Any obsessions or compulsions you have will take an even greater hold on your actions. The energy has to come out somehow.

Film Research

- *All That Jazz*
- *Barfly*
- *Cat on a Hot Tin Roof*
- *Crazy Heart*
- *Days of Wine and Roses*

- *Leaving Las Vegas*
- *Long Day's Journey into Night*
- *Lost Weekend*
- *My Name is Bill W.*
- *Under the Volcano*

Marijuana

Common substitutes for performances include herbal tobacco, and the tobacco from Ecstasy Cigarettes, which can be found at most smoke shops.

Methods and Timing

There are multiple ways of using marijuana, but the most common are in a pipe, as hand-rolled cigarettes – usually called joints – or in a water-pipe – known as a bong. It can also be cooked into foods such as pastries, brownies and cookies.

It's difficult to define the transition into the high that pot brings because it creeps up on you. One user described his experience this way:

"After you've had your first hit, you start wondering, 'OK, when's it going to kick in?' After a while, you realize that it's

already started. The transition is hard to identify. It's like trying to examine the moment of falling asleep."

Behavior and Rituals

- Eating snacks.

- Rolling a joint.

- Packing a bowl.

- Scraping the resin out of your pipe.

- Smelling the bag containing the pot.

- Caring for your own marijuana plant.

- Separating the seeds and stems from the leaves.

- Building your own miniature pot house with a sun lamp.

- Building a bong out of a soda can, apple, pineapple, water bottles, or a hundred other creative things.

Good Marijuana High

A good marijuana trip can be described as a transportation of reality, like going to another place. The drug provides a feeling of elation and contentment. Users often find themselves giddy and flooded with laughter. Your senses seem to become heightened. Physical and visual stimulants become more intense.

Food not only tastes better but also feels better in your mouth. There is a new appreciation for the textures and flavors that, in combination with a decreased feeling of being satiated, create the basis for the famous "munchies" effect – being hungry.

An increased appreciation of music, images, and nature is a major factor. Marijuana is often used as a creative tool for this very reason. Music sounds clearer, you have a more intense understanding of its elements, images appear more vivid, and you may feel a sense of oneness with your surroundings.

Creating the Feeling

- Pick your favorite happy color between lavender, pink, and orange.

- Let your body relax, releasing all tension.

- Imagine that your brain is gone and is replaced by a happy fog in the color you chose. Everything you think and see is through this misty haze of happiness. All problems are released and everything is chill. Look around and see the world through your misty, happy fog.

- Let your eyelids droop slightly.

- Improvise an inner monologue like the examples below or go to the script.

  - *This is good shit.*
  - *I'm just chillin', dude.*
  - *It's all good, man.*

- Optional: incorporate a giggle.

Bad Marijuana High

Because marijuana affects all the senses, a bad trip can be quite traumatizing. Users have reported distorted vision and hearing, lack of control over bodily functions or emotions, and a severely deformed notion of their environment. One woman described her experience this way:

"I felt like I was going to pass out and die, and I thought I'd never wake up... that I was in a coma or even dead dreaming the whole thing from the point we started smoking on the bench. I didn't know if I was alive."

Most bad experiences with marijuana are directly related to the fears, control issues, and insecurities of the user. Paranoia is a possible and tortuous effect of a bad marijuana experience. It is as though the world is judging you and conspiring against you.

Everything feels distant or possibly claustrophobic, conversation becomes difficult and there is an overwhelming need to simply stop being high. Movement can be difficult and reaction times are drastically slowed down. In some instances, when marijuana is mixed with alcohol, nausea and vomiting will occur.

Creating the Feeling

- Imagine your brain and body have been tranquilized.

- Give yourself a powerful **real life**, **50/50**, or **imagined** fear of death **trigger** (see the chapter on FEAR for more info).

- Let the rhythm of your breathing increase slightly.

- Improvise an inner monologue like the examples below or go to the script.

  - *Oh my God. Oh my God! I'm so busted. I'm going to jail.*
  - *Oh my God. I'm going to die. Holy shit. Fucking shit.*
  - *Somebody help me. I don't wanna die.*

Film Research

- *American Beauty*
- *The Big Lebowski*
- *Blow*
- *Bongwater*
- *Fast Times at Ridgemont High*
- *Laurel Canyon*
- *Pineapple Express*
- *Traffic*
- *True Romance*
- *Where the Buffalo Roam*

Documentaries

- *Super High Me*

Stimulants – Cocaine, Crack, Meth & Ecstasy

Stimulants, also called *uppers*, is a grouping that includes caffeine, nicotine, cocaine/crack, ecstasy, and methamphetamines. This section focuses on the latter three. These drugs are generally known for giving sensations of surging energy and euphoria, heightening sensory perceptions, sharpening the mind, decreasing inhibitions, and increasing sexual desires. Although there are many overlapping similarities, it is important to note that each of these drugs has a unique effect depending on the user, **environment** and dosage. Here we will explore the commonalities between these three drugs, then dive into the specifics of each.

Good Trip on a Stimulant

A good trip on a stimulant can bring various changes to peoples' emotional states and sensory perceptions. They will feel all-powerful, euphoric, extremely creative, open to others, and very sexual. A sense of intense clarity about the world will manifest and every thought will be a brilliant revelation, leading to excessive talking. Their physical energy will also peak and a warm rush will flow through their body. The surging energy typically results in a punchy, quick rhythm of movement and speech.

These are very extroverted drugs. Regardless of your personal situation at the time, conversation is dominated by the feeling that you're the smartest person in the room (or with ecstasy, that everyone is your best friend). This is not to say that these drugs make people feel serious. They are most definitely drugs of enjoyment.

Creating the Feeling

These exercises apply to cocaine, crack, and meth. Try them both and see what works best for you.

Exercise 1.

- Take a few strong breaths with vitality to get your body feeling energetic and alert. Try a few push-ups if you need an extra boost.

- Now give yourself the **as if** of an intense caffeine buzz. Feel your body's rhythm accelerate.

- Imagine that in front of you is a line of magic powder that will give you an instant, energizing surge of power, love, and intelligence. Now close on nostril with your finger and sniff the powder up the opposite nostril. Feel the intense rush. The energy and power is immense and it's filling your whole body. You're now invincible and intelligent beyond anything you thought possible.

- Get on your feet and physically express this new amazing energy and vitality.

- Imagine that your nose is drippy and that your mouth and the back of your throat have gone numb. Swallowing requires deliberate effort.

- Have an intense desire to talk about everything you know.

- Improvise an inner monologue like the examples that follow or go to the script.

Exercise 2.

- Take a few strong breaths with vitality to make your body feel energetic and alert. Try a few push-ups if you need an extra boost.

- Now give yourself the **as if** of an intense caffeine buzz. Feel your body's rhythm accelerate.

- Imagine that you're plugged into an outlet that's pouring orgasmic power, love, and intelligence into your body. It shoots into your chest, belly, head, groin and legs. It's a power that you've never felt before. It's **as if** you could solve all of life's problems all in one day.

- Stand up and physically express this new amazing energy and vitality.

- Imagine that your nose is drippy and that your mouth and the back of your throat have gone numb. Swallowing requires deliberate effort.

- Have an intense desire to talk about everything you know.

- Improvise an inner monologue like the examples below or go to the script.

    Inner Monologues

    - *You guys gotta try this. This is fucking amazing!*
    - *I love these people. This is so perfect, so amazing.*
    - *I can do anything! I can fucking do anything!*
    - *This feels so fucking good. I gotta call somebody!*
    - *This is so perfect. This shit is so fucking amazing!*

Bad Trip on a Stimulant (not applicable to Ecstasy)

Effects start small and can snowball into anxiety, fear, paranoia, paralysis, depression, and rage, any of which may trigger breathlessness or a full-blown panic attack. Excessive cocaine use can lead to formication, nicknamed "cocaine bugs" or "coke bugs," where the affected people believe they feel parasites crawling under their skin.

The user appears withdrawn, silent, visibly upset, scared or wild. Physical discomfort to the point of wanting to curl into the fetal position manifests. The user fears going insane and can become caught in circular thoughts, like a hall of mirrors.

Creating the Feeling

- Take a few strong breaths with vitality to get your body feeling energetic and alert. Try a few push-ups if you need an extra boost.

- Give yourself the **as if** of being on three times the amount of coffee you can handle. Know that if you can't slow down your heart, you will die.

- Give yourself a powerful **real life**, **50/50**, or **imagined** fear of death **trigger** (see the chapter on FEAR for more info).

- Let your breath quicken.

- Now you have insects crawling all over your arms and legs and under your skin. Try to get them off and out by physically scratching or picking them off.

> *WARNING: I recommend cutting your fingernails or using your fingertips for this exercise. You don't want to scratch yourself up like someone who's actually having a bad trip.*

- Improvise an inner monologue like the examples below or go to the script.

  - *Please God, no. I don't wanna die. Help me.*

  - *Oh shit. Oh my God. Help me. Please help me.*

  - *I took too much. I fucking took too much! Get these things off me!*

Withdrawal Effects

Primary symptoms may include:

- Fatigue.

- Anxiety.

- Irritability.

- Depression.

- Restlessness.

- General malaise.

- Suicidal thoughts.

- Increased appetite.

- Suspicion or paranoia.

- Vivid and unpleasant dreams.

- When cocaine use is stopped or when a binge ends, a crash follows almost immediately along with a strong craving for more cocaine. The craving and depression can last for months after the drug has left the system.

Cocaine

Common substitutions for cocaine in performances include Inositol (Vitamin B), powdered milk, and flour.

Methods and Timing

- Snorting cocaine typically produces peak effects within ten to fifteen minutes and sustains a high for approximately forty to sixty minutes.

- Injection produces peak effects within three minutes. The euphoria passes quickly.

Behavior and Rituals

- Fidgeting.

- Grinding your teeth.

- Flexing your fingers.

- Using a credit card to form lines.

- Dealing with your sniffly, runny nose.

- Putting the coke on your tongue to taste it.

- Rolling a dollar bill nice and tight to snort with.

- Crushing and smoothing the coke into a fine powder.

- Forming lines anywhere from an inch to an inch and a half long.

- Rubbing the small amount of cocaine left after snorting onto your gums for what's known as a "gum freeze."

Film Research

- *Addiction*

- *American Gangster*

- *Bad Lieutenant*

- *Boiler Room*

- *Boogie Nights*

- *The Boost*

- *Brick*

- *Bug*

- *The Departed*

- *Traffic*

Documentaries

- *Cocaine Cowboys*

Crack

Methods and Timing

- Both inhalation and injection bring peak effects in eight seconds and last for five to ten minutes.

- The injection process for crack is very similar to heroin (see the section on *Heroin* for more details), except that you dissolve the rocks with ascorbic acid, vinegar or lemon juice, add water, and then cook the crack at least fifteen seconds to prevent infection.

Behavior and Rituals

- Crushing the rocks into smaller pieces.

- Making a pipe out of a light bulb by using needle nose pliers and a screwdriver – search the internet for details.

- Playing with a candle or your favorite lighter. One addict's account described his lighter as his best friend in the world when he was high.

- Breaking the rocks into small pieces with a razor blade and putting them into the pipe.

- Heating your pipe.

Film Research

- *Addiction*
- *Bad Lieutenant*
- *Dope Sick Love*
- *Macarthur Park*
- *Notorious*
- *Paid in Full*
- *Traffic*
- *Training Day*

Meth

Methods and Timing

- Users who smoke or inject meth feel its effects after about eight seconds. Effects can last anywhere from two to twenty hours.

Behavior and Rituals

See cocaine.

Film Research

- *American Meth*
- *Boogie Nights*
- *Bully*
- *Cookers*
- *Crank*
- *Meth*
- *Methadonia*
- *Most High*
- *The Rules of Attraction*
- *The Salton Sea*
- *Spun*

Documentaries

- *Meth Madness: Teenage Methamphetamine Abuse*

Ecstasy (MDMA)

Also known simply as *E*, Ecstasy is different from the other stimulants in a few subtle ways. Typically, there is no bad trip. Instead of users feeling all-powerful, they feel intense love for all people and things. They express their love openly and experience empathy like never before. Strangers are their best friends. Withdrawals are typically a sore jaw and fatigue. While doing Ecstasy doesn't prompt a bad trip (unless it's not pure Ecstasy), it can be fatal just like any other drug.

Creating the Feeling

- Take a few strong breaths with vitality to get your body feeling energetic and alert. Try a few push-ups if you need an extra boost.

- Pretend that a heavy-duty power cord is hooked up to the middle of your chest and is filling you with optimism, hope, love, passion, and electricity. Feel it surge through you body. Look at the people around you and want them to feel it, too.

- Optional: add an intense oral fixation that creates the need to grind your teeth.

- Improvise an inner monologue like the examples below or go to the script.

  - *I love you so much. God, I fucking love you! This feels so good!*
  - *This music is amazing! This is the best music ever!*
  - *God, I fucking love this! I love these people!*

Methods and Timing

Ecstasy is generally taken in pill form. Effects hit in thirty minutes to an hour and last three to six hours.

Behavior and Rituals

- Dancing.
- Kissing someone.
- Rubbing someone.
- Listening to music.
- Grinding your teeth.
- Massaging a friend or lover.
- Relieving dry mouth with water.
- Chewing the inside of your cheeks.
- Stretching or massaging your own jaw.
- Sucking on a pacifier kept around your neck.
- Sucking or chewing on anything – straws, toothpicks, etc.

Film Research

- *24-Hour Party People*
- *The 51st State*

- *The Anniversary Party*
- *Be Angeled*
- *Berlin Calling*
- *Beyond the Valley of the Dolls*
- *Buffalo Soldiers*
- *Contact High*
- *Down in the Valley*
- *Go*

- *A Midsummer Night's Rave*
- *Party Monster*
- *Prozac Nation*
- *Reeker*
- *Rise of the Footsoldier*
- *Rolling*
- *The Rules of Attraction*
- *Severance*

Documentaries

- *The Chemical Generation*

LSD

Also known as *acid*, LSD is a strong hallucinogenic drug that gives the user a reflective, out of body experience. It's **as if** reality is suddenly uncensored, revealing a fantastically – and sometimes horrifically – distorted world.

Methods and Timing

LSD is most commonly packaged in pill form, as a sugar cube or on small strips of absorbent paper. All of these are ingested orally and normally take affect within thirty to sixty minutes. The high generally lasts four to six hours, but can persist for up to twelve.

Experiences with the drug vary depending on the amount taken, the user's state of mind at the time of ingestion, the setting, previous drug encounters, and expectations. The trip generally begins with jitters, racing heartbeat, nausea, chills, and numbness – especially of the face and lips. Then a distorted sensory perception kicks in, which may include illusions and hallucinations. These can range from heightened perception of the world around you – objects appear to breathe, flex, melt, glow, or change in size or apparent distance – to the composition of non-existent people or things.

Good Trip on LSD

Many users describe their experience as life-altering or religious. Often, at the peak of the trip, the user feels a greater sense of understanding, enlightenment, profound euphoria, and a feeling of wonder for the world.

How to Create the Feeling

- Close your eyes and imagine one of the following two options:
  - A wire from some point on your body is plugged into an electrical outlet that fills you with a current of child-like innocence and wonder for all things. Feel the warm energy flowing from the point of entry into the rest of your body.
  - A white light from above comes down to warm and fill your body with child-like innocence and wonder for all things. Feel it bathing you in warm energy.
- Open your eyes and look at your hands like you're seeing them for the first time. Look at the way your fingers move and wonder at how useful and magical they are. Look at your palms and take in all the lines and complexities. Flip them over and examine the veins that move blood all through them. Isn't it amazing that each finger is covered in skin that moves perfectly with your bones? Think about how fascinating your skin is and how it heals itself when you get hurt.
- Look away from your hands and look around the room **as if** you're seeing in color for the first time.
- Focus on one simple object in the room, such as a light switch. Marvel at its functionality, construction, the way it works, and how

it looks – its texture, color, shape, etc. You may think something like:

- *This is so weird. There's one in every room of this house, of EVERY house, and they're all connected like tree roots or vines. It's built like puzzle pieces or pegs that fit perfectly together. So perfect. It's so simple but has so much power. Enough to create light and heat. What's underneath this plastic thing? I want to take it off. It's probably just a bunch of colored wires. Oh my god. Colored wires! It's art. Beautiful and complicated. I flick it and the light comes on right away. It happens so fast. It doesn't need to think about it or work at it. Just BOOM. Light. The speed of light. Light travels faster than I can think. Light moves. Light can move. I can't hold light but I can move it. I can control light.*

- Improvise an inner monologue using the examples below as starting points or go to the script. Really delve into the object and explore it.
  - *This is so amazing.*
  - *Look at this thing! This thing is beautiful!*
  - *Whoa. So cool.*

Bad Trip on LSD

People having a bad trip tend to experience severe anxiety, increased heart rate, fear of death and fear of their surroundings. Users can hurt themselves or others because of their inability to think realistically about their actions. Someone tripping on LSD may falsely assume that they can drive safely or even fly.

Creating the Feeling

- Take a few strong breaths with vitality to get your body feeling energetic and alert. Try a few push-ups if you need an extra boost.

- Give yourself the **as if** that you drank way too much coffee. Feel the anxiety overwhelm your body.

- Give yourself a powerful **real life**, **50/50**, or **imagined** fear of death **trigger** (see the chapter on FEAR for more info).

- Imagine that your face and lips have been tranquilized.

- Add a feeling of nausea in your stomach. Taste the vomit of the food you've eaten today coming up in your throat.

- Imagine that the room you're in is locked and the walls surrounding you are those of a trash compactor and they're closing in to crush you.

- Improvise an inner monologue like the examples below or go to the script.

    - *Oh my god. Oh, fuck. Help me.*
    - *I'm going to die. Oh shit, fucking shit.*
    - *This is it. Oh God. Please God help me.*

Film Research

- *Across the Universe*
- *The Acid House*
- *Almost Famous*
- *Berkeley*
- *Bobby*
- *Bully*
- *Dream with the Fishes*

- *Go Ask Alice*
- *Harvard Man*
- *Party Monster*
- *The Rules of Attraction*
- *Thirteen*
- *The Trip*

Documentaries

- *The Beyond Within*

Opiates – Heroin

Opiates induce a dreamy, euphoric state, a decreased sensitivity to pain, pinpoint pupils and slowed breathing. Morphine, codeine, opium, oxycodone, meperidine, diphenoxylate, hydrocodone (Vicodin), fentanyl, and propoxyphene all fall under this category. Heroin, however, a chemically modified version of morphine, is the most abused narcotic of it's kind and will be the focus of this section.

Methods and Timing

- Injection gives the biggest rush of all the methods. The rush can last from forty-five seconds to a few minutes, followed by a period of sedation and tranquility that may last up to an hour. Users most commonly inject it into a vein – achieving the most rapid onset of euphoria in eight seconds – or else into a muscle or under the skin – allowing a relatively slow onset of five to eight minutes.

- Snorting and inhaling both bring peak effects within ten to fifteen minutes.

Behavior and Rituals

Most heroin users have developed routines of drug ingestion that vary depending on the environment and the user's socio-economic conditions. It is important to recognize that each user's method is subject to a great deal of patterning and stylization. An experienced heroin user can effortlessly, almost subconsciously, follow the steps.

Some users are known to carry a knife with them not only as a weapon, but also as a tool for handling drugs. A dealer uses a knife to scoop the drugs from his stash onto the balance or to eyeball the smallest sales unit, a halve streep (0.05 gram), at the point of the knife. A user may take the heroin out of the package with a knife and put it on the spoon for injecting or on foil for inhaling. The knife also acts as a status symbol. Most users carry small, easy to handle pocketknives, while dealers tend to carry larger daggers.

Injection

Required materials: a syringe, saline solution or distilled water, a metal spoon, a lighter, and a tourniquet – this could be a rope, belt, elastic band, or rubber.

- Mixing heroin powder with water in a spoon using the plunger of the syringe.

- Heating up the mixture with a lighter under the spoon until the heroin combines with the water into an even consistency.

- Putting a wet piece of cotton in the middle of the spoon, reinserting the plunger into the syringe and sucking the mixture into the syringe. Inverting the syringe, tapping the needle, and pressing in the plunger to squirt out any air bubbles (as injecting one into your blood stream could kill you).

- Finding a vein. If your character would inject into the left forearm, tie the tourniquet a hand's width above the vein you are going to use. Make a fist with your left hand and give the injection site a few small slaps. When injecting into your forearm, the needle should be pointing towards your elbow. Pull back slightly on the plunger to draw up some blood (this lets you know you are in the vein), then push in the plunger.

- Untying the tourniquet and removing the needle.

Inhalation

Required materials: a pocketknife, aluminum foil, a straw, and a lighter.

- Taking a knife-tip of heroin from the package and putting it on a strip of aluminum foil.

- Putting the straw in your mouth and taking the foil in your left hand, then bringing it about four inches from your face.

- Igniting the lighter just underneath the foil and allowing the end of the straw to hover over the heroin. As the heroin powder melts, it will turn into a dark reddish brown drop and start to run slowly along the length of the foil.

- With the straw, following the liquid and inhaling the fumes that curl up from it. When it approaches the end of the foil, stop heating it, but continue inhaling.

- Putting the foil back on the table and removing the straw from your mouth.

- After about ten seconds following inhalation, exhaling a relaxed breath of relief.

Good Trip on Heroin

Opiates cause a pleasant, lethargic state in which all worries are forgotten. It provides an orgasmic rush of pleasure, a feeling of absolute ecstasy, and then a sinking into a dreamy, blissful state, where you become detached from physical and emotional pain as well as any sexual desire or performance.

Creating the Feeling

- Sit in a chair and relax your body, letting go of any tension you may be holding, especially in your stomach.

- Blur your vision into soft focus. You may be able to do this without thinking about it. If not, either take your focus from what you're looking at around to the back of the eyes or find the balance between regular focus and having your eyes crossed.

- While in soft focus, lower your eyelids a bit, like you're extremely sleepy. It's **as if** weights are pulling them down.

- Imagine that tranquilizers have numbed your body and brain. Your body is melting into your seat, **as if** you've taken an hour-long bath followed by a perfect massage.

- At the point when the rush hits you, take a deep breath in through your mouth. As you exhale, feel a peaceful warmth come over you. It's **as if** you've had a wonderful orgasm followed by a feeling of absolute, perfect peace and love.

- Imagine that all emotional and physical pain melts away. Think of all the problems you struggle with and feel them dissolve away, one by one. You no longer have to worry about anything anymore. All your problems are falling away. Peace, love and bliss are yours. Finally, they're yours.

- Improvise an inner monologue like the examples below or go to the script.

  - *Thank you so much.*
  - *Oh my God, thank you.*

Bad Trip on Heroin

Users experiencing a bad trip on heroin often start to feel numb and begin to think that their heart is slowing down to a deadly rate. The feeling starts small and snowballs into anxiety, fear, paranoia, and paralysis. People experiencing a bad trip may appear withdrawn and silent or visibly upset, scared or wild. They may curl up into the fetal position. They feel like they're going insane and can become caught in circular thoughts, like a hall of mirrors. The anxiety may trigger breathlessness or even a full-blown panic attack. An overwhelming feeling of loss can also set in, as though the love of your life has died or left you. Jack Black gave the following account of his experience to *Blender Magazine*:

> *"I couldn't really feel my legs, and my heart felt like it was slowing down too much. I thought, 'Oh my God, it's going to shut me down. I'm going to die.' ...I had this strange sensation that my legs were pumping, but the feet were just sort of lifeless stumps."*

Creating the Feeling

- Imagine that your body has been tranquilized. Lower your eyelids, feel your nose begin to run and chills pass over your body. A violent sickness sets into your stomach.

- Give yourself a powerful **real life**, **50/50**, or **imagined** fear of death **trigger** (see the chapter on FEAR for more info). Your heart is slowing down too much. Something is wrong. The stuff you took is bad. Try to will your heart to beat normally again. Do whatever you can to live. Feel your heart slow down even more. Let your breath get heavier. Feel your body shutting down. You legs are going numb. Feel vomit coming up in your throat.

- Improvise an inner monologue like the examples below or go to the script.

  - *Please no. God help me. Please!*
  - *Snap out of it!*
  - *This can't happen!*

Withdrawal Effects

The early signs of withdrawal seem flu-like and are marked by moodiness, watery eyes, runny nose, yawning, sweating, restlessness and loss of appetite. However, as the time being off the drug increases, the symptoms become more intense and unbearable. The user suffers nausea, vomiting, diarrhea, chills, tears, aches and pains in the muscles and joints, abdominal cramps, insomnia, and muscle spasms in the legs that can cause them to kick. The worst of the physical symptoms dissipate after a few days but the craving for a fix can last for months afterwards.

Symptoms can set in as quickly as the recent dose wears off and usually peak between forty-eight and seventy-two hours after the last high. Within a week, withdrawal symptoms subside, although the user may experience some residual weakness and pain.

Film Research

- *Alpha Dog*
- *Candy*
- *Christiane F.*
- *Drugstore Cowboy*
- *Gia*
- *The Panic In Needle Park*

- *Party Monster*
- *Permanent Midnight*
- *Requiem for a Dream*
- *Riding in Cars with Boys*
- *Things We Lost in the Fire*
- *Trainspotting*

Documentaries

- *Dope Sick Love*
- *Heroin Addicts Speak*
- *Invisible*

- *Mum, Heroin and Me*
- *Turrets*

19

TRUSTING THE WORK AND LISTENING

You did the preparation. Now let it go.

The late Mali Finn, who was the head of casting for Warner Brothers when I was an actor, was one of those casting directors who really understood what we do. She was a fan of my work and called me in regularly. I respected her for a lot of reasons, but most of all because she was totally honest with her critiques. One day she said, "Let's try it again, less *soap opera* and more *lead in a film.*" Even though that was tough to hear, it felt okay coming from her because I knew she was trying to help me and was on my side. In other auditions, when I was stuck too much, she would say, "Let's run this outside," and then walk me out into the parking lot to do the scene. "Do it so that when people see us, they think we're in a real fight. Let's trick 'em."

It was a game to her. She would do her best to peel away actors' falsities and make them live the scenes. I always knew I could count on her to tell me the truth. The biggest lesson I learned from her came on an audition where I was down to the wire to play Robin in a *Batman* movie. She had said on a number of occasions that I was her pick and that she would put her neck on the line to fight for me. All I had to do was stand out and blow the producers away, and I would get the job.

While we were running one of the scenes, she stopped me. "Do it for the first time. I don't want rehearsal in here, so stop doing what you planned and do it today, Woolson!" We restarted the scene, and when we got a few lines in, she slapped me in the face just enough to startle me. "That! That's happening today. Do the scene!"

We ran the rest of it and even though I was shocked, I understood what she was trying to do. For the first time, I really understood. I couldn't give them the performance I had done in my apartment nor the one I wanted them to see. I had to invent it in that room. Yes, I had done the work, but I wasn't having any fun. The play and the improvisation were gone.

Years later, a client of mine went in to read for her. I warned him beforehand, "Watch out. She'll slap you if you don't listen and do it for the first time." He called me after the audition, and sure enough, he hadn't been "Mali Finn" present.

She had slapped him in the middle of his read and sent him off with a message. "Tell Woolson I said 'Hi.'"

Keeping the Work Fresh

The last part of the technique is to always trust the work, listen, and do it like it's the first time. It's always an improvisation within the framework of your choices. Be focused and more interested in reacting to your partner than you are in yourself. I realize that there are times in auditions when you can't exactly do this because you're dealing with a casting director that's eating a sandwich or reads in monotone. But you're there to deliver your choices to the best of your ability, so you must still connect with your readers and let them affect you. If you feel a bad attitude coming up, let that affect you, if it's appropriate. Just connect. Don't be a robot. No matter how good your choices are, if you just read the lines without connecting, it will come out without purpose or passion, and be a paint-by-numbers performance.

When you let go of the work and connect the judgments and concerns of how you're coming off will disappear. You'll be in the zone. You won't do it like you did in rehearsal. You'll simply pursue your **objective** in each moment. If you mess up in an audition room, don't sweat it. Mistakes are often gold and make the work more authentic. Some of the biggest jobs my clients book are from auditions where they mess up a line or two, and the execs don't care. A mistake can make you more present, so go with it, not against it. If you ever start over in an audition, it should be because you're not listening or connected to the material, the reader, or the here and now. That's when you're in trouble and beginning again may save your performance.

Being in the moment means exploring your choices. Sometimes you literally have to tell yourself before you go on stage or into an audition, "I'm going to do this like I've never seen these lines before." This is what I was missing as a young actor. I was so terrified that when I would mess up, I'd cling to my choices like a life raft instead of being free. Always be prepared to abandon any pre-conceived ideas you have for your character for new ones that may arise in the moment. The idea is to get into a state of effortless flow.

People in my class often hear me say, "Were you listening?" Why? Because it's one of the most important ingredients of great acting. Sanford Meisner knew this, which is why he came up with his famous repetition exercise.

Are you being affected by your partner or are you just saying lines and picking up your cues? Good listening goes like this:

• Your partner says a line,

• You have an emotional reaction,

- You have a thought,

- You respond with a line.

If this is something you have difficulties with, do your best to find a teacher or colleague that will call you on it. When actors who have trouble listening come to coach with me, there are a few methods I use to put them back on track. The first is simply to remind them to listen and to be affected by what's happening moment to moment. If that doesn't work, I'll have their partner improvise and change the dialogue slightly so that they'll have to listen and find an appropriate response. A third method is to have the actor repeat a *key* word or phrase in their partner's line before they say their line. So let's say your partner's line is, "How could you do that? How could you sleep with my best friend?" And your line is, "Where did you hear that? I gave her a ride home, that's all!" After your partner says, "How could you sleep with my best friend," you might say, "Sleep with? Where did you hear that? I gave her a ride home, that's all!"

If after trying these methods, you still have trouble listening, enroll yourself in a program that does Meisner work. You must master this skill. **Listening well and being affected by what you hear and sense is fundamental to excelling at this art form.**

Think of it this way: acting is like playing tennis. You can't focus on the crowd or think about how you look when you hit the ball, nor can you try to re-enact the game you played yesterday. You have to focus on the ball coming at you in that moment. The minute you lose sight of it, you lose the game; the minute you go up into your head, you're not watching your scene partner anymore. I always tell my clients, "Do all the work you know how to do and get your performance from your partner."

When prompted to speak about the freedom she seems to have as an actress, the great Helen Mirren had this to say to interviewer Peter Eyre:

"Yes, that was always how I wanted to be on stage. I wanted to be free, a sense that it was being invented then and there in front of your eyes, and that it wasn't a performance that was

rehearsed. But you go through endless machinations and torture to try and get to that point if you're doing many plays, especially classical plays, because it's incredibly technical. You can't avoid that fact. It's like being an opera singer. You've got to get that down and then find your way into the freedom beyond it. You can't have freedom without technique. I've always said one of my great inspirations as an actor was Francis Bacon, the painter, who spoke brilliantly about really what acting's all about. I mean, he happened to be talking about painting. He was talking about the struggle between technique and accident. Ultimately every child is a brilliant painter because it's all accident. But Bacon goes on to say that you can't draw like a child when you're thirty. It is no longer interesting. It becomes false and stupid. So you have to inevitably learn technique, and then you struggle with that technique because you want to get back to the freedom of a child. And then, he says, you come out the other side where your technique is so well in place that you can afford the accident because you know what is a good accident and what is a bad accident. And that's so true about acting."

I often quote Mirren as talking about this freedom, though I had forgotten that she referred to Bacon. Interestingly enough, Bacon got the idea from someone he looked up to, Pablo Picasso, who had this to say:

"Every child is an artist. The problem is how to remain an artist once he grows up."

Enough said.

20

AUDITIONING

Creative and professional choices.

The best actor with the right look for the role books the job.

While the above statement is generally true, there are a number of other things that can help an actor in the audition room. Be aware that the following points are guidelines and can be abandoned in certain circumstances. You, as the artist, will have to carefully judge when to do so. That being said, here are some of my beliefs about what works and doesn't work in the room.

Dressing as the Character

Wear something comfortable that suggests a flavor of the character without going over the top. If your character is very conservative, wearing jeans with holes in them would not be as smart as wearing a preppy shirt with pressed pants. On the other hand, if you're auditioning for a soldier, you don't want to go in camouflage with your face painted; you might scare someone and will almost certainly look like you're trying too hard. A tight, khaki-colored shirt and jeans or cargo pants will suffice. If you're playing a princess, a ball gown would be probably be perfect on set, but ridiculous in the casting office. If the character happens to be similar to you, wear what you feel confident in. Either way, you shouldn't draw more attention to your wardrobe than to your performance. The exception would be for a final callback where your instinct tells you that you can go for it. Sometimes it can be just the edge you need to win a role.

Note to women: Avoid showing too much skin. It's distracting and it screams of desperation. If you're playing a sexy character, strike a balance that says you understand the essence of what the character would wear, but that your performance is enough to earn the part.

Props

For the most part, props are not needed in the audition room. The exception is anything that would be reasonable for you to have in your purse or pockets. Whenever there is a phone needed, it's best to use your cell phone – making sure, of course, that it's on silent. If you write something down, use a pencil. Compacts with mirrors are simple and can work if they are put away quickly. Cigarettes can be okay if you don't light them. As an actor, I once had an audition for a guy who was building a bomb, so I brought a battery and two wires to fiddle with. It gave me **behavior** at the top and I put it all away when I was done with it. On the other hand, I once had a student who wanted to bring a real gun into an audition so he could clean it. Anything like that could be dangerous or viewed as unprofessional. At the very least, it could definitely be distracting for the casting director.

Whatever it is, make sure that you don't use it so much that you stop listening and being present with the other person in the scene. If it takes over your performance, it's not good. Less is more. Here's the basic rule for props in auditions: sometimes a small one can help you enormously, but in general, keep them to a minimum.

Pitfalls of Miming

When an actor mimes in an audition, it has the tendency to immediately draw attention to the reading as being false or fake. I usually say, "No miming," but there a few occasions in which it may be necessary, like quick mimes that don't draw attention to themselves. Tossing someone an imaginary set of keys is a simple example. Things that are okay to mime – and are sometimes necessary – are guns, cigarettes, and phones – this being only if you don't have a cell phone with you, and it's best to shape your hand like you're holding a phone, not in the thumb and pinky *hang loose* gesture. There are rare occasions when a character is playing a sport like basketball and is commenting on what he is doing in the dialogue. In these cases, you may find it necessary to mime. Whatever you decide, keep it creative yet simple.

Prepping for Tears

In regards to scenes that involve tears, I advise slightly welling up your eyes by using your **trigger** once or twice a few minutes before performing – whether you're in the waiting room or backstage – so that when the emotion is needed, you've warmed up your instrument. Be aware, though, that you must never fully reveal the emotion until it's needed in the material. After bringing it up slightly, go back to neutral and enter the scene with the appropriate **moment before**.

When presented with an audition that features a light scene followed by one with heavy emotion, you can do one of two things. If you're worried about going into the difficult scene after the easier ones, just ask if you can read it first. Most casting directors will let you, and if they do, you'll be able to launch into the scene easily after having prepped in the waiting area. If reading the scenes in order works for you (or if casting doesn't let you do the difficult one first), just take a moment to prep before the difficult scene, centering yourself and letting your **trigger** come up. You'll want to be sure, though, to have a strong choice so that it can come up quickly – no more than five or ten seconds.

Entering the Audition as the Character

My answer is yes and no on this one. Yes, bring the part of you that is most like the character you're playing. If you're normally very outgoing and you are reading for a shy character, you need to tone down your personality a little bit. If you're more on the reserved side and you're reading for a character with a big personality, adopt that energy when you walk into the room. Don't be fake; simply be your most extroverted self.

If your character is from Moscow or happens to have Tourette's syndrome, don't enter the audition room with a Russian accent or ticks. You are an actor and they will be more impressed when they see you morph. So, go in with a flavor but don't be afraid to let them see who you are first.

Physical Interaction

Any scene that involves a physical interaction with another character can be challenging. My experience has taught me that it is best to connect to the energy of these things rather than try to fully recreate them physically. In cases where you're supposed to hug, kiss, or otherwise sexually interact with the character opposite you, a simple **intention** like *to kiss* or *to comfort* can do the trick. Likewise, if you're supposed to shove someone, a simple move forward with the **intention** of pouncing or attacking works.

You may come across stage direction like, "She takes her shirt off." A **verb** choice with a simple physical move can be very sexy. For example, if you are wearing a tank top, pushing one of the arm straps off your shoulder or even unbuttoning a sweater with an **intention** of *tempting* is enough. You can even wear layers that you can take off and put on the back of your chair, as long as you feel comfortable and have a shirt on underneath, of course. Maintain your integrity while being brave and specific.

Nerves

Many actors worry about nerves and there are a few ways to handle them. The first involves removing your focus from yourself and noticing a detail in your environment. This method helped me quite a bit when meeting powerful people in my teens and early twenties. I would often become so nervous that my bottom lip would shake and my body would tense up. Then, one of my teachers taught me to take a second and find a detail outside of myself. From then on, whenever I felt nervous, I would notice something about the person that I wouldn't normally see while in a state of fear – like a mole, the color of their eyes, a piece of jewelry they were wearing – and I would calm down. You can even look down at your own hand and notice a detail like a scar or a vein. Taking a couple of subtle, deep breaths while doing so will also help. Then go back to looking at the person and you will likely feel calmer. This technique takes your attention off of yourself and helps you become present.

Another technique involves making friends with the nerves, seeing them as energy to be used and put into your performance. The truth is that all great performers have been afraid, even those who have won Academy Awards. So, since it's unlikely that you'll ever rid yourself of your nerves entirely, you might as well see them as fuel. The fact that they show up means you care.

Yet another way to calm nerves is to walk into auditions with the **as if** that you've just booked a big lead opposite Anthony Hopkins (or some other big star). I used to do this when I was an actor and it would often give me more confidence. After all, I was already doing a movie with Anthony Hopkins. This guest star lead I was auditioning for was just icing on the cake. Maybe for you, it would be better to use the **as if** that you're going to do this little audition and then head out to a romantic dinner with one of your favorite celebrities. Regardless of what or whom you choose, this is a playful way to calm yourself.

The thing to remember is that nerves usually aren't as apparent as you think they are, either. The people around you can typically only see a fraction of what is going on inside. So, stop taking them so seriously and they will stop sabotaging your work.

Talking with Casting

This can be confusing for many actors. Remember that directors, casting directors, producers, and everyone else in the business are just people. Feel free to ask them intelligent questions about the material if you're confused about something. Subjects that are not related to acting are fun, too, as long as they are not downers. Keep things positive and talk to them as a real person. The vast majority of them don't want to be worshiped; they want to be able to see you as an equal. Sometimes you'll come across casting people who are on power trips or who don't want to talk. Don't take these things personally. Just do your job the best you can and leave. Just because they don't want to talk doesn't mean they hate you. Perhaps they're tired or behind schedule. They may also have personal problems going on that have nothing to do with you.

Feedback

Don't get caught up in what a director or casting director says to you after a read. They can say all sorts of things. Some of it will be true; some of it will just be polite. Cultivate the ability to be your own judge of your work without being too hard on yourself. If you felt you did your best, that's what matters. If you receive specific feedback from casting or your agents, good or bad, take it in and see what you can learn from it. Negative feedback can sometimes be just what you need to get a fire under your ass to work harder. Of course, some negative feedback is destructive and unhelpful. Know how to tell the difference and remember that in the end, opinions are just opinions. If you didn't get a callback, either you weren't as right for the part compared to the other people that went in, or you simply weren't good enough. The latter is likely more accurate and all it means is that you have to work harder and smarter.

Moving on

Do not hold on to projects after you have read for them. Whether you feel they went really well or horribly, let them go. I am repeatedly faced with clients who think an audition went incredibly well, then end up hearing nothing and are heartbroken; and others who beat themselves up for giving a poor audition and then book the job. Focus on the next audition or working on your weaknesses in class. Holding on to what might happen can cause stagnation and make you very bitter in the long run. Do not call your agents repeatedly for feedback. This comes across as desperate and is a waste of your energy. Spend that energy on the next creative project instead. Keep a positive attitude, stay present, move forward, and enjoy every moment of your life.

"Choose Two Scenes"

If casting gives you four scenes and says "pick two" – or something similar – simply pick the scenes you like the best that you think will play to your strengths. Take into consideration the time you have to prepare and the difficulty of the scenes. Don't pick the hardest scene if you need more time than you have. If you're a quick study and the difficult scene is something you think you can nail, go for it. I also think it's important to pick two scenes that have very different energies. If the first scene you want to do is light, pick a deeper one for the second scene. Remember that the goal is to get the callback.

Attention: do not schedule a coaching session and ask your coach to pick the scenes for you. This is a cop-out and keeps you from doing the critical homework needed to have an effective coaching session. Arrive prepared with the scenes you have chosen.

Signing Your Work

Do your best to put your mark on your performance no matter how good or bad the material happens to be. Make choices and bring your personality to everything you do. They're not looking for perfection; they're looking for an interesting, creative person. Phillip Seymour Hoffman said, "*Auditioning's a whole different beast... It's actually a moment of just throwing down and trying to see what you can bring there, 'cause you haven't evolved the character [yet].*" [6]

If you're not excited about what you have to offer to the material, no one else will be. Get pumped up about your choices and your chance to act. This can't be faked. You either really love acting or you're a poser. If you can't find something exciting about an audition that comes your way, don't go. Your agents may hate me for saying this, but the truth is that if you hate the material, it will probably come

---

[6] Tichler, Rosemarie, and Barry Jay Kaplan. *Actors at Work.* New York: Faber and Faber, 2007.

through in one way or another. If you subject yourself to this pattern for long enough, the passion will be sapped from your work. Don't get me wrong; I think it's possible to find something to like about almost anything if you really want to. A horribly written soap opera can be a fun challenge in making the bad dialogue sound good. Even a cheesy horror film can be emotionally challenging.

Be careful that you don't pass on things because you're intimidated by them, and know that the feeling of "I'm better than this material" is often fear in disguise. You must look deep inside and be honest with yourself. Do not be pressured by agents and managers. You are the one who has to do this stuff, not them. It's your career.

Talking to More Than One Character

We've already discussed how to deal with **objectives** when talking to multiple characters in a scene. In an audition situation, you must also consider where to place these characters, and there are two ways to do it. The first is to simply allow the person reading with you in the room to morph into all the characters in your mind's eye. Since it's so important to connect to the casting director, this is often the way to go and is most effective when you talk mostly to one person.

If you have only one or two lines to a side character, feel free to look a few feet to the left or right of the reader for those lines; there may even be someone sitting a few feet from the reader who can receive these lines. If you find yourself talking to the air for too long, find a way to go back to the reader.

If an additional person in the scene is a sidekick who could easily be placed next to you, feel free to speak as if that person was standing by your side, keeping in mind that it's best if this look is kept as brief as possible.

When you're talking to a crowd of people, focus mostly on the reader, and then create specific characters on either side. Be sure to send most of the lines to the reader once you have established the crowd. And again, if there are more people in the audition room, like in a producer's callback, using them as part of the crowd can be very effective.

Memorizing & Landing Lines

It's almost always acceptable to hold the audition pages (usually called sides) in auditions. The only times when it's not a good idea is when you're doing a screen test of some sort and they want to see you fully prepared. To be clear, during first calls you need to have your lines memorized as much as possible. You can use the pages, but not as a crutch. During a screen test, you must be 100% off-book.

My rule about **cold reading** – auditioning for something you've had only a few minutes to prepare – is to avoid it whenever possible. Why half-ass something when you could do it fully? Unfortunately, casting people are known for reading actors for one character and then deciding to immediately read them for another. On some occasions, you'll even get that last-minute call and not have time to memorize the material. In these situations, you must forego learning the lines. Just go straight to the technique (doing as much work as you can on **objective**, **emotional relationship**, **moment before**, and **background**) and be sure to land the lines.

Landing lines is the simple technique of making eye contact at the end of key sentences. It doesn't matter if you're looking down at the paper for the rest of the line as long as you put your **intention** into the paper as if it were the other character. You mustn't break from how you feel about the other person just because you're not looking at them. If it's a flirty scene and your **intention** is *to tease*, keep that **intention** even when you're looking down. Once you've read ahead enough to be able to look up and finish the sentence, do so with the **intention**. If the line is, "When you talk like that, it makes me want to kiss you," it will be a strong read as long as you're up with your eyes on the words, "want to kiss you." The problem arises when people look down for the end of the line or immediately after landing it. There is a moment at the end of sentences when that connection happens. Practice this. It is a skill that can be mastered over time, but don't rely on it. Memorizing lines is usually ideal.

Being Creative with the Paper

A good thing to think about is that there are times when you can use the sides creatively. The most obvious involve scenes wherein a character interacts with something like paper – reading a magazine, handing someone a letter, pointing to a place on a map, etc. In these cases, the sides can replace the item. A client of mine once had a scene where he was supposed to be working on a model airplane. I had him fold up his sides into a paper airplane and then continue making smaller folds to refine it.

The pages can become so many things. Not only can they represent a magazine, letter, menu, photo, diploma, book or map, but they can also be rolled up to represent a bat, barbell, golf club, or peppermill. Turning the page can even signify opening a gift box. In cases where it turns into something when you roll it up, it's a good idea to casually unroll it when that part of the scene is over.

Sitting or Standing

If the character is sitting in the scene, sit; if they're standing, stand. Of course, sometimes sitting down for scenes where your character stands is fine, like for walk-and-talk scenes. The point is to use the room as needed. If the character sits through the scene then stands at the end to leave, do that. If the character walks in at the beginning and then sits down, do that. If all else fails, do what makes you feel most confident and engaged. Use the room while keeping your choices as simple and authentic as possible.

Keeping Your Ego in Check

Everyone has an ego; that includes you and it includes me. Anyone who says they don't have an ego doesn't understand what the ego is. The ego is the part of us that says we are better than a certain job or actor. With acting, the ego tells us that the business owes us a something. The ego says it's unfair that 'that guy' booked the role because we have more credits or are better looking or have more talent. The ego tells us we are better because we study with a certain coach or hang out with a cool group of people. The ego is jealous and is constantly comparing and keeping score. The ego is the voice inside that tells us that we're done learning. Ego doesn't want to help move the furniture between scenes in a scene-study class. Ego says it's okay to be lazy since we're so far ahead. Ego wrecks peoples' careers for them. Ego is the un-evolved, selfish part of us, and the more successful we become, the more it wants to prove its case. It wants us to believe that self-confidence and humility are opposites, when in fact, they are much closer than we think.

Be confident, humble, and focused.

21

REHEARSAL RULES

Making the most of your time.

"In English, the word for rehearsal *derives from rehearsing. In French, rehearsal is* la repetition, *and it means what it sounds like: a repetition. My favorite meaning comes from the German,* die Probe, *which sounds like what a rehearsal ought to be: the probe! I want to probe, to test, to try… to adventure."*

– Uta Hagen

Rehearsals need rules. Here are a few:

1. Don't chitchat about agents, auditions, relationships, or anything else that's irrelevant to the material until after the rehearsal.

2. Don't waste your partner's time or your own. Do as much technique work as possible before showing up to rehearsal.

That means having read the material at least once and jotting down all notes and first instincts. The dialogue does not have to be memorized, but be familiar with it. Even for the first rehearsal, be careful not to get stuck in the way you say your lines. Try out different **objectives**, **triggers**, and **intentions**.

3. During your second rehearsal, show up with lots of ideas and choices. If the scene isn't working, stop it and try another choice. Use the rehearsal to find out what parts of the scene need deepening. Remember that it exists so that you can take big risks and find out what works. This is part of the fun. Then go back home and work on any bits of the technique that need attention.

4. Before doing the work in class, be sure to have read the script two or three times so you can garnish as much of the writer's intent as possible. Every time you read the script, you'll find something you missed before, which will give you a more intimate understanding of your character. All the facts are there. It's your job to discover them.

5. Do work in class with the same dedication you would bring if it were a paid job. I've seen so many students get jobs based on the recommendation of another student who was impressed with their professionalism in class.

6. Take the work seriously, not yourself. Step back once in awhile and look at the bigger picture. It's about progress, not perfection, whether it's in regards to your rehearsals, your career, or your life.

7. Do not give your scene partner advice about the way they're playing their character if they don't ask for it. Focus on your own work. If what they're doing isn't working, be sure your teacher is the type to point that out. On the flip side, don't be so set in your independence that you can't mention the things you need help on to make the scene better.

8. Work hard, be on time for rehearsals, and don't complain or make excuses. Be a pro. **Keep practicing and honing your craft until the work appears effortless**.

9. Leave the workspace or stage at least as clean as you found it. That means putting away furniture you used and cleaning up any trash. Respect the space.

22

HAVING A BALANCED LIFE

Your career isn't everything.

Please have a life outside of acting. I don't mean work less. I mean have other things going on. If you're one of those people who's desperate for show business to give you a job so you can feel validated, guess what? The business isn't going to help you with that. So pursue fun things and make sure you work your ass off. I have said that if you aren't spending at least two hours a day on acting, you're not an actor. I stand by that, but I would like to add that spending *all* of your time on acting isn't healthy either.

If you're the type who tends to be lazy, I'm not talking to you. You may not use this as an excuse to take a vacation or blow off whatever you need to do. I'm talking to those of you who *obsess* about working hard. Ease up. Have some fun. Take those guitar lessons or those singing lessons you've always wanted to take. Paint a picture. Travel to another country. Get out there and fight for a cause you believe in. Do *something* for your own personal enjoyment and don't let your whole identity be reduced to acting. This business and the people in it can easily induce frustration or disappointment. **Despite cultural myths, the more projects you book, the more you will realize that happiness truly has to come from within.**

So, don't look to show business to give you a life, solve your problems, or remove your pain. Have a life and the business will find you. In short, stop asking for blessings and instead be one.

23

EMOTIONAL FOCUS WARM-UP

Releasing tension to prepare for scenes.

This is a good exercise to use before an audition or performance. It will allow you to warm up your instrument so you can execute your triggers with greater ease, particularly on those days when you're working on highly difficult material. The first few times you go through it, you may want to start with your eyes closed and then open them once you start your **trigger-work**. Eventually though, you'll want to practice with your eyes open so you can prepare no matter what's going on around you. The goal is to be able to enter that zone whether you're backstage, in a make-up chair, in a waiting room for an audition, in your trailer, or even when the crew surrounds you and you're about to do a take.

1. Start by getting into a comfortable position. Sit down, avoiding anything too cushy that you would normally sleep or relax in. Put your feet flat on the floor and let your hands and arms relax at your sides or on your thighs.

2. Focus on your breath. Concentrate on your inhale and exhale with the goal of letting go of any thoughts that may be distracting you. If a distracting thought enters your head, that's okay, just keep going back to the breath. It can be helpful to say to yourself, "Breathe in, breathe out." After a minute or so, when you feel that you are somewhat centered, focus on your feet and take four to six breaths. On each exhale, release any tension you might be holding there. Continuing in this fashion, move slowly and deliberately through your legs, pelvic area, glutes, stomach, chest, shoulders, arms, hands, neck, jaw, face, and eyes, along with any other unmentioned areas. Pay particular attention to your stomach, shoulders, neck and jaw. Be aware that along the way, you may become emotional. This is due to the fact that whenever we avoid fully feeling emotions in our daily lives, we tend to store them as tension in our muscles. If a feeling comes up, simply let it happen and move to the next area when you feel ready. Once you've covered your entire body, you may want to go back and focus on particularly tense or stubborn areas. You might even want to massage or move those areas in a particular way. Always remember, if you begin feeling frustrated or stuck, go back to the breath. Don't pressure yourself too much. Do what you can and move on.

3. Now allow your body to move the way it wants to move, simply expressing externally what's going on internally. It doesn't need to be pretty. If you're feeling angry, you may punch out; if you're happy, you may jump up and down with your arms in the air; if you feel goofy or silly, you might move your hips around and flail your arms. It may be that if someone were to watch you do this, they might think you're crazy. No worries, this exercise is for *you*. Again, if a feeling comes up,

that's a good thing. It means you're more open and alive. You're ready to start the work.

Note: There may be times in your career when the movement portion will not be appropriate, like in a make-up chair or on a set. If you know you're going to be in this type of situation, go through the exercise before you begin your day or simply omit the third step.

If at any point in the exercise you feel as though there's nothing going on with you, it's likely that you're either judging the exercise, or that you're a bit blocked from what's going on in your life. Being open and free can take some practice. Keep going back to focusing on your body and your breath. Sometimes it can even help to think about the fact that this exercise isn't working for you and then express how that makes you feel. After you've finished, you should have less tension and be more open, more alert, and ready to work.

24

GENERAL TICKS

The habits you hide behind.

Find a teacher that will call you on your **ticks**. **Ticks** are repetitious movements or cliché gestures that actors will do when they don't know what else to do. These movements are usually completely irrelevant to the scene and reveal themselves in times of insecurity or generality. Your job is to find a way to identify your own **ticks** and eliminate them. You may have to be in your head for a bit of time, but it's worth it in the end. When these general habits are stripped away, more authentic and less distracting moments of **behavior** will arise in their place, better serving your work.

Some of the most common ticks include touching parts of the face, allowing the hands to fall and slap the legs, raising the hands from neutral to a palms-up "I don't know" position, running the hands through the hair, licking or puckering the lips, sighing, making a 'tsk' sound, bobbing the head, excessively pointing a finger, shifting weight from one foot to the other, turning one foot to the side, looking away while shaking the head, etc.

These gestures typically come from bad habits and/or the lack of specificity with **objectives** and **intentions**. If you find yourself pleading with open hands for too long, it often means you need to be more active. Instead of using the energy of *Can you please give me what I want?,* commit yourself to doing what is necessary to get what your character wants.

If you don't have a class or teacher that calls you on these things, you can always discover them on your own by filming yourself while acting. However you go about it, do this work. **Body language** is amazingly powerful and eliminating your ticks can take your career to the next level.

25

BE YOURSELF. NO MORE, NO LESS.

Embracing your authentic self.

It's a statement that people often dismiss as something that doting mothers say. "Yeah, I know, be myself. Blah blah blah." But let's explore this a bit. If you're not the leading lady, get out of the fantasy that your career is going to take off in that direction. If you're an okay-looking person, be an okay-looking person. I know: how dare I say something like that. But the truth is that we are only beautiful when we stand firmly in what we truly are.

Have you ever seen a guy who's trying to be more than what he is? He's fifty-five, driving a sports car, wearing designer clothing that someone half his age would wear, trying to pick up twenty year-olds, and showing off his face lift or hair plugs. It's like he's saying, "I'm not old, bald, or okay-looking. I'm a hot, rich, thick-haired, young stallion." The truth is that he's not fooling anyone. Wouldn't your opinion of him be more favorable if he accepted his real age and appearance? This is an extreme example, but almost everyone does it on some level.

Consider this: is the purse you carry or the watch you wear part of your self-esteem? Do you find yourself telling people that you have more going on than you really do? Can you afford the car you drive, or is it out of your budget and you're holding onto it to appear more successful? Are you real with yourself about your talent level?

Thinking of yourself as less than you are can be just as limiting. Are you playing your looks down? Do you physically shrink in auditions because you think you're too tall? Do you give yourself enough credit? Do you brush it off when your friends tell you that you're talented? Are you negative when you talk about your ability as an actor?

Trying to be something you're not can be very off-putting, so be honest with yourself. If you come to me thinking that you're amazingly talented, a simple note like "Listen more" will bounce right off of you. Something inside of you will say you're too good for simple exercises. That's your ego talking and it needs to be looked at. **The irony is that the very thing we're trying to cover up is often the thing that will make us interesting to others.**

Think about a woman who wears way too much make-up. Too much make-up always says, "I'm trying to be more than what I am." Older, younger, prettier, etc. A woman who stands in her truth simply says, "I am." That is beautiful. So, stand in the reality of who you are. *I'm bald. I'm old. I'm young. I'm still learning.* Stay away from denying your insecurities. People who do this are uncomfortable to be around because they're lying to themselves and the rest of us. Many celebrities who aren't what you'd call classically beautiful are, in fact, charismatic and very watchable. Why? Because they have (for the most part) embraced themselves, flaws and all. Look at Will Farrell. He stands in the fact that he looks like an ordinary guy and plays leading roles.

This doesn't mean you shouldn't *strive* to become something more than you are, to ascend to something greater than what others would expect for you, but do so truthfully. You'll be surprised to find that when you embrace who you are, the world will seem to say 'Yes' to you. So what are you waiting for? Be what you are, no more, no less.

26

SUCCESS STORIES

There's no business like show business.

When I was an actor in my early twenties, I wasted a lot of time being jealous of other actors who seemed to have everything come to them really easily. I struggled with insecurities, money issues, and was always working my ass off in class. Every now and again, I would hear about these people that, without any apparent effort at all, would get a big break. The first few times this happened, I really drove myself crazy. *Why am I working so hard? Why is it so easy for them? How did they get so confident? Poor me. I have to work my ass off while they, with their charisma and good looks or whatever, make it look easy. I wish I could be like them.*

There will always be people that make it look easy, but guess what? You don't want to be these people. Why? Because they typically don't have amazing careers. They either slide by on their talent until no one wants to hire them again, or they become known as a hack who only does it for the money. Yes, there are some exceptions where people have success early on and go on to have amazing careers, but that's only if they do the work. For the most part, people who are always hired because they know how they look, how charismatic they are, or whatever, never get to feel the joy of ascension and love for what they do. After all, it's easy for them, and although that may sound desirable, challenges and growth shape us as artists and as human beings.

That brings me to another point: every single one of us will be challenged in life. Even if someone has instant success, they'll have other obstacles to address. It's like people who are born rich. They have their own set of problems and pain. **Money can't buy true happiness and luck can't bring lasting fulfillment**. So the next time you feel jealous of someone because they're on the fast track, see it for what it is: a mirage that will soon vanish if they don't do the work on themselves and their craft.

I hope for your sake that you're not an instant success or, if you are, that you take the time to attend classes, do theatre, or work in indie films. You'll have a greater appreciation for your peers, more easily avoid the need for rehab, and be better off in the end.

Bouncing Back

A friend of mine asked me to meet him for coffee. Let's call him Bobby. He was depressed. His girlfriend had just broken up with him and although he had worked as an actor before, it had been over a year since his last job. He couldn't afford to stay in his apartment and was behind on the rent. He was thinking of quitting acting and becoming a songwriter. I knew how talented he was as an actor. He had an amazing work ethic.

Two weeks later, he called me and said he had booked a TV show. The money was good and he wouldn't have to move out of his apartment after all. Three months later, he was on the front cover of *Entertainment Weekly.* I remember looking at the magazine and thinking, *This is so weird. Just a few months ago, he wanted to quit and now he's a star.* Six months later, his show was a huge hit and he was buying a house. A year after that, he met the girl he would end up marrying and his show won an Emmy. Five years later, he was the highest-paid actor in the history of dramatic television. We sat down for coffee a few years ago and laughed. The show had offered him thirty-three million dollars for three more years. **It's a strange thing, but when things seem the most difficult, you may be on the verge of making your biggest leap forward.**

Getting Dropped

The next time your agency threatens to drop you or gets on your case about not booking jobs, remember this story.

I once had a roommate whose agency dropped him for receiving bad feedback from an audition. He later signed with a better agent and worked even harder to prove himself. He went on to become a huge star and is still working today. The agency that dropped him is out of business.

Struggles with Representation

Another friend of mine, David, struggled through most of his twenties trying to find representation. He had to deal with panic attacks and a severe learning disability that made reading difficult, so he had to memorize his dialogue for every audition. He had a horrible relationship with his father, who constantly told him he was stupid and good for nothing.

He teamed up with his first agent at twenty-eight. He worked hard and eventually booked enough commercial work to make a living as an actor in his thirties. Years later, he was cast as a lead in one of the most respected shows on television. He now has his own show opposite an academy award-winning actress. So what's the moral of the story? Having a hard time finding representation doesn't mean you can't rise to the top.

Hard Work Pays Off

Joanne was struggling. She was a character actress with a ton of talent and no auditions. She made jewelry for extra money to pay the rent and was $30,000 in debt. She owed her agent another $5,000. I remember that when she wanted to buy something, she would have to try several different credit cards because most of them would be declined. She loved theatre though, and was always doing a play at some small venue in town.

In one particular production at the Zephyr Theatre, she played a wonderfully comedic character with a high voice that she had come up with for the role. Years went by and we lost touch, but eventually I heard Joanne was doing a play on Broadway and was up for a Tony Award. A few years after that, she booked a lead role in one of the most successful sitcoms of all time, playing the character she had created ten years earlier for the play at the Zephyr.

Getting Fired & Getting Cut

When I was an actor, I had a friend in class who was cast as a series regular and then was fired without being told why. It devastated her. She got another big break when Steven Spielberg cast her in a movie he was directing. Unfortunately, every scene she was in ended up on the cutting room floor. Later that same year, she was cast in another show, only to be fired because the execs didn't like the chemistry she had with the romantic lead. One day she came to class in tears. "What's wrong with me? Fired! Cut out! I'll never make it in this business."

Out of frustration, she decided to produce and star in a play. After all, she wasn't going to fire herself. However, even after several valiant attempts, the writer denied her the rights. Just when she was about to give up acting, she received a call out of the blue that Spielberg wanted to make it up to her for cutting her out of his movie. He gave her a leading role in his next picture. She was finally on top. When the movie debuted, she enjoyed wonderful reviews and eventually went on to star in her own award-winning show that has been running for seven seasons and is still going strong.

Bad Feedback Isn't Always Fact

Jenna's biggest credits were B-movies from the eighties and 90210. A producer told her agent that he couldn't test her for a big pilot because she wasn't strong enough to play the lead in a dramatic series.

She didn't give up. She got mad and used that anger to propel herself into an amazing role in an independent film. Less than a year later, she won an Academy Award for Best Actress, and then another a few years later.

†

All of these people have tremendous work ethic and perseverance. I hope they have inspired you and reminded you that we all struggle and have **obstacles** to overcome, but as long as we pick ourselves up and work hard, we can do amazing things.

27

BAD DIRECTION

How to safeguard yourself.

You're on the set of a movie-of-the-week and the director, who thinks he's Scorsese, pulls you aside. With a far-off look in his eyes, he summarizes the plot for you in a tone of voice that suggests you're supposed to think of it as revelatory. "So, Chris. Here's the thing. The character of 'Jack' is a bus driver. Right? And every day he drives a bus, okay? Then, one day, he meets this girl and she just blows his mind. Turns out, though, that this girl is a bank robber. And in this scene he finds that out, right? You get me? So try it more like that. Oh, and you can go bigger this time, especially on 'bank robber'. And pick up the pace a bit."

If you're in this situation you may think this guy has no idea what he's doing or, at the very least, he doesn't understand the technical process of most actors. Rather than saying all that out loud, it's best to hear him out and see how you can use strong acting choices to give him what he's asking for. After all, that's part of your job as a professional. Just make sure that you don't fall into the trap of result-oriented acting or indicating.

Directing is a high-pressure job and even the greatest can resort to giving bad direction when they're racing against time or are unable to effectively communicate their vision. Try to have compassion in these moments and remember they're doing the best they can with the tools they have. Sometimes you'll need to stand your ground with your choices, but remember that blowing up on the set or acting like a diva is never appropriate. Doing so will only create tension, a toxic work environment, and a bad reputation for you. Always use your best judgment and trust your creative instincts.

Know, however, that fighting for your choices doesn't apply to auditions. Sometimes during the casting process, they just want to see if you can take direction, regardless of whether it's right or wrong. Just know that if you don't give them what they want, you are less likely to get the job.

So, since it is inevitable that you will be given bad direction at some point, I've included this chapter in an effort to empower you to change the confusing direction you receive into something you can use. Below is my *Bad Direction Glossary*, filled with some common directorial faux pas. It's important to note that not all of these examples are actually bad direction. Some are simply notes that actors are sometimes confused by, but all of them are things that were said to me or to people I know.

Know also that if a director doesn't give you adjustments, there's no need to worry. This often means you're on the right path. Typically, great directors hire the most talented actors they can find and let them do their thing, only giving subtle feedback as needed.

Direction	Translation
Do it like this: "(line reading)."	Give them a flavor of what they want without losing your own voice or your ideas about the character.

Speed it up.	Raise the **stakes**. You have to want your **objective** more. It can help to give your character a place they need to be (the store, a special date, etc.), thereby moving the scene along.
Slow it down.	Listen more, take your partner in more, and don't overplay your **objective**. Let it breathe and don't speak so fast.
Angrier/More mad.	Raise the **stakes**. Go after your partner more. Find stronger **verbs**: *punch, smash, obliterate, kill, destroy, scare, crush, castrate, disturb, impale, conquer, pulverize, terminate, terrify, torture, slaughter, punish, massacre, intimidate, exterminate, corner.* Another effective choice is to try to anger the other actor in the scene rather than *being* angry.
Do (generic action) *on that line.*	If possible, justify the move and then just do it. If you're having trouble, ask the director if he or she can justify the action. Sometimes film is technical. Don't fight it. Just do your best to make it natural.
Be sexier.	Find more playful or sexier **intentions**: *Titillate, thrill, tantalize, stimulate, pleasure, nibble, lick, impassion, excite, entice, arouse.*
Great, but this time, I want the tears sooner.	Do your best to **trigger** yourself sooner but don't fake anything. If you have a physical **gesture** that helps you get to the feeling, go to it sooner.

More intense.	Try stronger **intentions** that will give you that quality: *threaten, interrogate, disturb, stab, scare, terrify, intimidate, or on the more positive side, invigorate, energize, inspire, ignite, impassion, thrill, motivate, stimulate.*
More colors.	Bring more interesting **intentions** and possibly find some lightness or humor.
Just say it/ Just throw it away.	Stop acting. Back off your homework and be simple. Remember to listen. Less is more.
Bigger.	Be braver in going after your **objective** both verbally and physically.
Do it monotone.	Strip your performance down to simplicity and back off the **objective** significantly.
Do it a bit different this time.	Ask them if they can be specific. If they can't, let your instincts choose.
Be real.	Stop acting and start listening and reacting in the now. Tune down your **objective** but don't throw it away.
A little looser.	Relax and let it go more. You're hanging onto your choices too much.
Be more surprised.	Give yourself an **as if** that is more surprising and find a task that you can focus on before the surprise moment so you don't anticipate it.

More passion.	Go after your **objective** more. Raise your **intention** choices.
Be more black/ *More street/* *More urban/* *More* (any nationality).	This can be an extremely offensive piece of direction. I think it's really a question of deciphering whether the director is asking you to be more of a stereotype and deliver a "ghetto dialect," or if they want you to be tougher. If it's the latter, just employ **intentions** that have that vibe. If it's the former, here's what to do: think of someone you know well in real life or who you've seen in a movie or show who has that quality and bring that person into your performance rather than doing an exaggerated caricature across the board. The "ghetto dialect" can be tricky for people who don't do it naturally. Swiveling your neck or sucking your teeth is all surface level parody and should be avoided whenever possible with the exception of certain forms of comedy. Another way into a deeper interpretation is to determine when this character might react in a more guarded or defensive way than you do. If this is a note you hear a lot and you have a desire to do this type of work, try studying great films that have the quality you're looking for.
More warmth.	Find more love and compassion for the character you're in the scene with.
Do more.	Simply go bigger with what you're doing while staying authentic.

Be younger.	Resist all temptations to play at being young by affecting your voice or face. Instead, try using the **as if** that this is the first time you've been through something like this.
More energy.	Bring more vitality into your performance by going after your **objective** more. One trick I often use with clients is to have them do some push-ups right before starting the scene.
Be more scared.	Raise the stakes and go to a stronger visual image of what will happen if you don't get what you want in the scene. See the chapter on FEAR for more info.

I hope this helps you survive bad direction. Remember, sometimes you'll come across an actors' director who knows what he or she is doing. When you do, these notes need not apply. Regardless, always do your best to enjoy the work and know that this business is built on collaboration. There's nothing worse than actors who won't listen to notes because they think their way is the only way. Every on-set experience should be handled uniquely based on the skills and experience of the people involved. **Humility, flexibility, and honesty are often the best tools for a smoothly running set**.

EPILOGUE

Loving the process.

Acting is a demanding art that involves tremendous dedication. Just reading this book will not make you a great actor. You must find a platform and put these tools to work. If you're kind to yourself and others and commit fully to the process, you will be amazed at what you can accomplish. Like a beautiful life, great acting is born not out of talent or privilege, but from a strong purpose and a love for the craft. Bottom line: do the work and eventually someone will want to support your talent. Michelangelo was known to have said at the peak of his success "I am still learning". It has always been true in my life that ascension cultivates happiness. You are not simply a rudderless boat on a river that takes you endlessly downstream. You have the power to continually shape and transform your life into a masterpiece.

My challenge for you is to see the completion of this book not as the end but as a new beginning. Stay humble and grateful, and let your actions have boldness in them. Life is happening now. This is not a dress rehearsal!

I hope this book has been helpful in deepening your craft. I encourage you to return to it when needed as a reference tool for any character you might play. Once again, enjoy the process and reward yourself often. Lastly, never forget your life is more important than your career. Don't ever let your self-worth be dependent upon where your career is at any given time. Your true value must come from within. So, I will leave you with the words of one of my favorite poets, Khalil Gibran...

"You are far greater than you know and all is well."

Appendix A

SCRIPT ANALYSIS REMINDERS

The homework.

- **Given Circumstances:** What are the facts and clues the writer has given me that I must honor when building my character?
    - Where does the scene take place?
    - What time is it? What season? What year?
    - Who is in the scene and what facts do I, as the character, know about them? What are my relationships to them emotionally?
    - What do I, as the character, know about myself – my attitudes, my background – that is relevant to the scene?
    - What do I say about myself as the character? What do the other characters say about me? Given what the script tells me, are those things true?

- How do the other characters treat my character?
- What literally happens during the scene?
- What events or conversations have taken place – or have not taken place – that are relevant to the scene?

- **Super-Objective**: What do I want that drives me from the beginning of the story to its end?

- **Objective**: What do I want from the person(s) I'm talking to that drives me from the beginning of the scene to its end?

- **Stakes**: How high are the **stakes**? What will happen if I don't get what I want?

- **Emotional Relationship**: What is my specific relationship to the person(s) I'm talking to?

- **Moment Before**: What relevant events lead up to the scene, how do they affect my character emotionally and physically, and how am I going to get there?

- **Emotional Triggers**: Where are the emotional moments and how will I connect to them?

  - What is the event by which I need to be triggered?
  - What might the character be feeling because of that event?
  - How am I going to get there using **real life**, **imagination**, or **50/50**?

- **Inner Imagery**: What persons, places, objects and events in this script need to be endowed with specific emotional **backgrounds**?

- **Intentions**: What are the methods I use to get what I want in the scene?

- **Obstacle**: What's standing in my way of getting what I want?

- **Physical Behavior**: What **physical behavior** can I bring to reveal who my character is and what my true motives are?

- **Humor**: How can I bring humor or lightness to this particular role?

- **Destination**: In the scene, **where** does my character move and why?

- **Environment**: How does the place affect me emotionally and physically?

- **Character**: Do I need an **accent**?

- **Character**: What **song** can I use to prepare myself for playing this character?

- **Character**: What is my character's **body center**?

- **Character**: What is my character's **worldview**?

- **Character**: What particular **animal** embodies the energy and **physicality** of my character?

- **Character**: Do I have any **psychological gestures** that say something about who I am?

- **Character**: Does my character have any **secrets**?

- **Fear:** How do I create **authentic fear** for myself for scenes that require it?

- **Comedy**: What is the **style** of this project?

- **Drugs**: How can I embody the **effects** and **behavior** of my character's drug of choice?

- **Trusting the Work**: Remember to listen and do it for the first time.

Appendix B

REMINDERS FOR INTENTIONS

- Most playable **intentions** fit into the sentence *I _____ you.*

- Use active **verbs**, not inactive **verbs** or adjectives.

- Use **intentions** that allow you to do something to the other person, not to yourself.

- Use specific, workable **intentions**, not general ones like to *explain, tell* or *ask.*

- Choose **intentions** that create physical impulses, whether subtle or bold.

- Look for places to use lighter **intentions** where other actors might only use heavier ones.

- Break the rules when it's appropriate.

Appendix C

FIFTY CHARACTER QUESTIONS

Questions to ask yourself as the character.

The following are fifty questions to ask yourself as the character. Do your best to come up with answers that **trigger** you emotionally.

1. In what city and state were you born and when?

2. What are the five most common active **verbs** that you use to get what you want in life?

3. What type of humor cracks you up?

4. What are three situations that would bring you to tears?

5. What do you do for work?

6. What do you love about each of your family members?

7.　What is your favorite spectator sport?

8.　What is your favorite sport to participate in?

9.　What is your favorite TV show?

10. What would put you into a rage?

11. What is your favorite color?

12. What is your political affiliation?

13. Do you gamble?

14. Do you have children? Do you like children?

15. What religion do you practice and how do you feel about it?

16. What's the most exciting thing that's ever happened to you?

17. What is the scariest thing that has ever happened to you?

18. How are you brave?

19. Describe your house or apartment.

20. What diseases have you ever had and what were the effects?

21. Have you ever been in love? When and with whom?

22. When and where was your first sexual experience?

23. Do you smoke or drink?

24. Do you take drugs or have you ever?

25. What are your life goals? Name three.

26. What is your strongest physical attribute?

27. What do you least like about your appearance?

28. What are your strongest and weakest personality traits?

29. What piece of music would soothe you?

30. Who in this world would you change places with?

31. How do you react to heavily emotional situations?

32. Are you more of an aggressive or passive person?

33. If you could change anything in your life, what would it be?

34. What is your **body language** like?

35. What are your favorite foods?

36. How would you describe your sex life?

37. What newspapers/magazines do you read? Which section of the paper do you go to first? (i.e. comics, business, sports)

38. What is the most recent book you've read?

39. If you could be any kind of animal what would you choose? (This is different from the animal that represents you)

40. How do you dress?

41. How do you hide your feelings?

42. How do you feel about death?

43. How do you get along with people in general (at home, at work, in romantic situations)?

44. What is your secret shame, if anything?

45. Why don't you want to die?

46. What contribution do you want to leave for the world?

47. What do you feel about your education?

48. Who is your hero in life or from history?

49. What is your relationship to money?

50. What is your greatest pleasure?

Appendix D

REMINDERS FOR COMEDY

Comedic guidelines.

- Get into a playful mindset.
- Identify your character's **comedy core traits**.
- Know whether you're playing the funny one or the straight one.
- Research your material to find out as much as you can about the size and tone of the show, film, or play. Is it 4-camera or single-camera?
- Explore and create physical choices.
- Remember that comedy is heightened life.
- Stick to the script. Observe all punctuation and don't change the dialogue unless invited to do so.

- Let the rhythm of the scene be like that of a tennis match. Eliminate pauses that are not specified by the writer. Get to the ends of the lines with vitality.

- Remember your replacement emotions for sitcom: *heightened frustration* instead of *anger* and *overwhelmed* instead of *sad.*

- Come up with **thoughts** before all lines.

- Mine the material for places to inject **reversals, recoveries, over-articulation** and **covers** where appropriate.

Appendix E

FURTHER READING

ACTING

A Challenge for the Actor by Uta Hagen

Emotion on Demand by Michael Woolson

Freeing the Natural Voice by Kristin Linklater

The Intent to Live by Larry Moss

Method or Madness by Robert Lewis

On Acting by Sanford Meisner

BEING AN ARTIST

The Artist's Way by Julia Cameron

The Creative Habit by Twyla Tharp

Letters to a Young Poet by Rainer Rilke

Making Movies by Sidney Lumet

Notes on Directing by Hauser and Reich

The Right to Write by Julia Cameron

A Sense of Direction by William Ball

Story by Robert McKee

The War of Art by Steven Pressfield

BUSINESS

The 9 Steps to Financial Freedom by Suze Orman

Acting is Everything by Judy Kerr

The Courage to be Rich by Suze Orman

It Would Be So Nice If You Weren't Here by Charles Grodin

Rich Dad, Poor Dad by Robert T. Kiyosaki

The Wealthy Spirit by Chellie Campbell

HEALTH AND SUSTAINABILITY

The Better World Handbook by Jones, Haenfler & Johnson

The Detox Solution by Dr. Patricia Fitzgerald

The Kind Diet by Alicia Silverstone

Self-Help

7 Habits of Highly Effective People by Stephen R. Covey

The Dark Side of the Light Chasers by Debbie Ford

Do You! by Russell Simmons

Dreams into Action by Milton Katselas

The Four Agreements by Miguel Ruiz

How to Argue and Win Every Time by Gerry Spence

A New Earth by Eckhart Tolle

The Prophet by Kahlil Gibran

The Road Less Traveled by Scott Peck

The Seven Spiritual Laws of Success by Deepak Chopra

You Can Heal Your Life by Louise L. Hay

ACKNOWLEDGMENTS

My wife, Rachel Avalon, for her editing skills, creative ideas and for reminding me that love is all you need. Braden Lynch for his friendship, relentless dedication to this book, sense of humor, and his talent as an actor and coach. My mother for her absolute truth, never-ending courage, and all the times she told me anything is possible. My father for his kindness and passion for architecture and all things old. Ralph Pine, my publisher, for his integrity and his belief in this book. Larry Moss for his guidance and wisdom over the years. Russ Savage for being a second father and showing by example what it means to give unconditionally. John Meyer for being my best friend and making me laugh at least once a week for over twenty years now. Sharon Ressing, for always believing in me and paying for my first acting classes. Don and Edith Woolson for being the spirit behind my art and work. Haldane Morris for his truth, friendship and sense of humor. Josh Zuckerman for his inspirational work on the stage and dedication to the craft. Michael Connors for his wisdom and creative contribution. Anson Mount for helping me to find my clown. Amanda Fuller for being fiercely brave and for giving my wife a best friend. Di Quon for her willingness to rally behind the dreams of others. Bert Hilkes for his feedback and kindness. Mark Cappellano for his friendship and integrity. Kenny Johnson for giving me a model for bravery and tenacity. Annie McElwain for her patience and dedication to making this book look beautiful. Dawn Reynolds for being the best mother-in-law a guy could have. George Caldwell for his never-ending support. John Wasko for being a great father to my wife.

Breck Costin for breaking my paradigms and telling me the absolute truth. Milana Vayntrub for her important creative contribution in the beginning stages of this book. Gregg Foster for building my theatre and helping my dreams become reality. Most importantly, to all of my students, who give me much more than I will ever give them: It's because of you that I get to do this.

The following people have helped me in both subtle and significant ways. Your dedication and/or belief in me over the years means more than you know.

Aaron McPherson, Abby Pivaronas, Adam Griffin, Adam Levine, Alex Cobo, Allison Scagliotti, Amanda Schull, Amy Handelman, Anne Woodward, Arash Haile, Ashley Rickards, Beau Hodges, Beau Mirchoff, Ben Bonnet, Bjorn Johnson, Bobby Naderi, Brantley Brown, Brian DePersia, Brian Drillinger, Brian Watkins, Cali Fredrichs, Carolyn Thompson-Goldstein, Charles Carroll, Cheri Steinfeld, Chris Edwards, Christian Meole, Cindy Osbrink, Constance Marie, Daisy White, Dallas Sonnier, Danna Brady, Danna Edric, Danny Devito, David Eisenberg, David Mamet, Dee Ann Newkirk, Devon Werkheiser, Diane Venora, Dustin Varpness, Eileen Stringer, Emily Woolson, Francesca Cecil, Gill Hodgson, Grandpa & Grandma Rush, Hailee Steinfeld, Herb Deer, Ira Rubin, Isabella Blaine, Jacqueline Brown, Jake Carpenter, Jakki Jandrell, Jamar Brown-King, Jean-Louis Rodrigue, Jeanine Mason, Jenna Flexner, Jeremy Hogan, Jesse Allis, Jessica Williams, Jill Latiano, Jimmy Cundiff, Johanna Ray, John Ritter, Jon Robertson, Jonathan Keltz, Jonathan Sacramone, Jonny Wexler, Josie Lopez, Julie Dretzin, Justin Deeley, Kahlil Ashanti, Kaitlin Cullum, Karl Wiedergott, Katherine Brunk, Katija Pevec, Kenneth Dolin, Kenneth Probst, Kimberly Horner, Kyle Gallner, Kyle McKeever, Laura Morgan, Lauren London, Lisa Passero, Lisa Robertson, Lizz Rantze, Loch Powell, Lucy Devito, Lukus Grace, Matt Fletcher, Meredith Fine, Michael Welch, Michelle Horn, Mila Kunis, Mitchell Gossett, Molly McCook, Molly Quinn, Monica Bugajski, Nancy Banks, Neil LaBute, Noah Wylie, Noela Hueso, Orie Rush, Peter Kluge, Phe Caplan, Philip Leader, Ramsey Krull, Richard Roat, Robert Easton, Robert Haas, Robert Thompson,

Ryan Surratt, Samantha Krutzfeldt, Sarah Foret, Sarah Shyn, Scott Fish, Scott Wine, Shoshana Bush, Susan Curtis, Susan Nickells, Ted Schachter, Tia Marrie, Tiffany Thornton, TJ Stein, Tom Connolly, Torrey De Vitto, Travis Van Winkle, Tyler Williams, Valarie Miller, Whit Thomas, and my sisters.

INDEX